Madison Taylor

M000099608

MARIE TAGBO

How I Became a Teen Actor

Everything You Need to Know About Starting Your Teen Acting Career

First published by Marie Tagbo 2019

Copyright © 2019 by Marie Tagbo

All rights reserved. No part of this publication may be reproduced, stored or transmitted in any form or by any means, electronic, mechanical, photocopying, recording, scanning, or otherwise without written permission from the publisher. It is illegal to copy this book, post it to a website, or distribute it by any other means without permission.

Marie Tagbo asserts the moral right to be identified as the author of this work.

Marie Tagbo has no responsibility for the persistence or accuracy of URLs for external or third-party Internet Websites referred to in this publication and does not guarantee that any content on such Websites is, or will remain, accurate or appropriate.

Designations used by companies to distinguish their products are often claimed as trademarks. All brand names and product names used in this book and on its cover are trade names, service marks, trademarks and registered trademarks of their respective owners. The publishers and the book are not associated with any product or vendor mentioned in this book. None of the companies referenced within the book have endorsed the book.

First edition

This book was professionally typeset on Reedsy.
Find out more at reedsy.com

Contents

Introduction

Hi! My name is Marie Tagbo. Thank you so much for picking up this book. I have titled it "How I Became a Teen Actor: Everything You Need to Know About Starting Your Teen Acting Career." Wheww... Try to say that ten times fast.

(Headshot by Elizabeth Wiseman Photography)

I just want to say how glad I am that you have found this book. I remember when I was staring out in this industry. I was young, excited, naive, and overwhelmed by all the available information. And I was doubtful. Could I start a career without living in Los Angeles?

I thought most actors had to move to LA to be successful because every famous actor I knew did. LA is where most television shows, films, and web series are filmed and cast. I had so many questions. Who do I trust and put my money in? How does one get an agent? Do I have an appealing look for casting directors? I had all so many puzzles to solve and no answers.

My journey to star in local films, TV, and commercials was complicated. I learned the hard way: step by step. I started my career by stringing together scattered bits of advice from the internet. I learned from experience. I got scammed, ran into pitfalls, made mistakes, wasted money, and remained unaware of crucial pieces of business advice for months.

Since then, I found my way. I learned from my successes and failures. My career has included countless theater productions and auditions. I have done paid and non-paid film and commercial work all over the Midwest for years.

My specific credits include but are not limited to a lead role in a local Super Bowl commercial, a lead in a docu-drama on human trafficking, producing and starring in a Christmas short film, meeting local filmmakers, interviews, doing fashion shows and more.

I eventually got an agent, networked with professionals, booked commercials, auditioned for Disney and Amazon, and established a successful local career. I have done all of this while living in the Midwest, where film tax incentives and opportunities are low. But I have managed to create opportunities through the resources and help available to me.

Although I am glad for my journey, it was an inefficient one. I would have loved a book like this book. In this book, I will share tons of audition stories and career mishaps. I provide countless concrete tools for getting your career together and getting in the casting door. This book is thoughtful and packed with information. It will not only impact your career but your life as well if you take these words to heart. I am so happy to be part of your journey. I know it will be as rewarding for you as it was for me.

Disclaimers

Before continuing further, I want to clarify that I am not a Hollywood Industry expert. I have written, and researched every part of this book on my own, and proofread it endlessly but I know that I am not without mistakes. Consider this book's imperfections a testament to its authenticity. Feel free to let me know about any grammar mistakes, spelling errors, and unfinished sentences that are inevitably in this book. And I hope that my rawness does not take away from its message.

My second disclaimer is that I am not an acting instructor. This book does not provide formal methods of script analysis or the deets on how to deliver an Oscar-worthy performance. I *will* tell you how to find the correct acting training, and I will give you approaches to breaking down a script. But this book is not an instruction manual on the actual craft of acting itself. The skill of acting can not be learned by reading. You must act.

Lastly, if you are looking for me to guarantee you success and notoriety, this is the wrong place and the wrong career. If I could ensure fame and fortune, I would get it for myself. What this book offers is a detailed and thorough guidebook for teen actors, written by a teen actress. This book is guaranteed to give you filled the kind of advice that will launch your career, and place you miles ahead mentally of the rest of your competition. I will answer ever burning question you have in this book, and after reading you will be completely prepared to begin a successful acting career wherever you live. But how far you go is entirely up to you.

About Me

Hi. My name is Marie Tagbo. I began writing this book when I was fifteen, and now I am eighteen years old. I am an actress, YouTuber, 2nd-degree black belt, and now I guess a writer. I was homeschooled from ages 5-14, which I did so I could pursue my career. In freshmen year, I started my current online high school, Stanford Online High school.

I started theater when I was nine, and I began film-acting in early 2015. When I started acting in 2011, I pursued it casually, with I had no expectations. But I am so thankful I tried it because my acting career has granted me many exciting opportunities and projects.

I started my YouTube channel right after I began film acting. I now help other aspiring actors follow their dream through my videos. I have been able to do amazing things on my channel like publish short films, film acting how tos, and interview my mentor: Wendy Alane Wright. I am so thankful for every subscriber. They are so supportive of my film work. They have watched me grow up, and they are always there for me. So if you are reading this, and you subscribed -

If you are not subscribed, move on!!! Now that they are gone... Hi and thank you! You inspire me to keep going. I would never have been able to write this book if it were not for you guys. I hope to encourage you with my work and hand you all the tools to follow your dreams, wherever you may live.

If you are not subscribed, stop what you are doing RIGHT now and check out my channel: https://www.youtube.com/c/marietagbo

I never imagined that I would be doing all these things, but I have learned that with God, all things are possible. I truly owe it all to him. God has always been there through my darkest moments. He has shown me that through a belief in him, a big dream, research, creativity, and preparation, you can do things that you never imagined.

Your potential is limitless, and your future has hope. You are amazing. It is time for every teen to recognize that!!

Writing This Book

Although I made acting videos, trained for years, and successfully established my career, I never thought of myself as a teacher. But as I became more open about my acting career on social media, the questions flooded in. Everyone wanted to know, "Marie, _**how**_ do you start an acting career?"

My mom, who I am so thankful for, encouraged me daily to write a book. I constantly wondered, "Why would teens want this book? I am not a superstar! What can I offer teens?" But she believed in me, and she pushed me to move forward. And so many people had questions for me that I felt forced to write. As I wrote and wrote, information came tumbling out.

I realized that I have learned from every experience and every piece of advice out there. I have amassed a treasure of wealth, of insider advice, and have so many stories…

So upon completing this work, I can finally say with confidence that this book is valuable. This book will show you how to begin your acting journey. I give you advice here that you will never find anywhere else. I am an open book, and in this book, I talk about _everything_. You will know how to become an actor, and you do NOT have to live in LA or have connections or an impressive resume. I will show you how do it. Study this carefully and Enjoy,

Marie Tagbo

A Brief Overview of Film Terms

In this book, I will use film terms that may be new to you. After a while, these terms will become your second language. But for now, here are their definitions, so you do not have to Google every 5 seconds.

Cold Read: A cold read is when you are reading from a script in class or an audition with little to no rehearsal or familiarity. You are going into the text "cold." If you get an audition script less than 24 hours before an audition, that is typically called a cold read.

Sometimes in a cold read audition, you will be handed the script AT the audition. You will not be expected to be memorized for a cold read, but I suggest coming in as memorized as you can! If you get the script more than 24 hours before the audition, you are expected to be memorized.

In a cold read, you prepare for the character using only the information from the script and the casting director. Cold reads can be scary, so in Chapter 27 we will talk about how to ace your cold read audition.

Breakdown: "Breakdowns" and "Casting Calls/Casting Notices" are used synonymously. A breakdown is the "breaking down" of the project. It is the description of the project, and it gives you information about:

- The company.
- The audition and filming dates.
- The film's union status.

- The pay rate.
- The characters and their descriptions.
- The story's logline.

In the character's description, you can find what race/age/type/skills are needed to play each part. Read everything in the breakdown to know whether you are eligible to submit for a role.

Callback: Any audition after the first audition is the callback. Because they "called you back" ...haha.

Callbacks are good signs because when you get a callback, it means that the casting director likes you and thought you fit the role. You proved to them that you are talented and can work on their set.

Once you get to callbacks, the casting process is out of your hand. They are looking at small little details to choose the actor for the role. They look at height, chemistry with the other actors, and the opinions of the director/producer. All of these are factors that are out of your hands.

Demo Reel/Performance Clip: Demo reels are clips of your acting work from previous projects you have done. It may be hard to get the footage of yourself acting so you hire videographers to help you shoot a scene. You can also ask local filmmakers and photographers if they are willing to shoot a scenes for you for free.

A performance clip is a thirty sec to one minute clip of you performing a scene or monologue and showing your best acting. You can create a performance clip yourself.

For newer actors in the business, industry experts suggests putting together 3-4 performance clips that represent the kinds of roles you would be cast in. Post your performance clips individually on your on your website, your social media, and acting profiles. Actors Access first shows casting directors actors who have paid to upload their demo reel, performance clip, or "Slateshot" (a video of an actor slating).

Your clips should only focus on your acting skills, and it should mostly have close up shots of you talking. Do not include scenes with someone who looks like you.

Marie Tagbo Romantic Comedy Monologue

One of my most recent performance clips, filmed with Creative Actors Studio

Headshot: A headshot is an 8x10 photo of you that **EVERY ACTOR** needs. A headshot focuses on you, shows your acting type, and capture your essence. You bring your headshots with you into auditions. I suggest having three extra copies of your headshot with you with your resume stapled on the back.

You will have different headshots that to submit for different kinds of roles. You use a more serious photo for a drama project than you would for a comedy or commercial. More on headshots in Chapter 10, 11, & 12.

Resume: A resume is a singular piece of paper with your experience, contact information, and acting training. It lets casting directors know almost everything about you concerning your acting career. They can see what roles you have played, what *types* of roles you play, and your contact information! A resume also includes your talents, training, and unique skills. Your resume must be formatted neatly and correctly. In Chapter 8 & 9 I show you how to format your acting resume.

Casting Director: Casting Director or "CDs," have a misleading name because they are not a director or an agent. They are hired by a director/producer to find actors and host auditions. In indie and low budget projects, the film director/writer is also often the casting director. But directors prefer to hire casting directors, because they have relationships with agents, managers, and actors that they can trust. They are the ones who create a breakdown and send it to agents and managers, or put it publicly on a place like Actors Access.

Agents and managers submit headshots of actors they represent who an actor who fit the role. If the breakdown is available to actors, the actors submit their headshot and demo reel. The CD (or the casting intern) weeds through the submissions talent to find talent who might fit the part. Those who they feel fit the role get called in to audition. The CD brings a small percentage of people who auditioned in the first round for a callback. Then the casting director might have a hand in helping the director select his final choice.

In summary, the casting directors direct the casting of a film. CDs determine who gets auditions, who gets a callback, and who the director should see. However, they often do not get to make the final decision on casting choice.

Casting Intern/Assistant: Casting interns work for and with a casting director. Their job can range in importance. They may be the ones who go through piles of headshots or answer the phone, or read the partner's lines in an audition, or get the CD coffee. They are there to learn from or assist the CD.

Director: The film director directs what happens on set. They turn the screenplay into a movie. They visualize the project, and organize the crew and cast together. They ensure that the production runs smoothly. They have the artistic vision and use it to direct the actors, the cinematographer, and the other crew members.

In many low budget projects the directors will often have two or more jobs, like writing or casting etc, because they do not have the resources, money or time to hire someone else.

Production Assistant: Production Assistants are also called "PAs." They assist in production. Their job can be an umbrella term, and can it refer to a set intern or the director's right-hand man (also called Assistant Director). They help organize and communicate with the actors. They may watch for continuity with the script, gather the required supplies, set up and take down, and create overall safety.

Gun Wrangler: The gun wrangler is the person who oversees the use of any gun, real or fake, on a set. They ensure that safety precautions are being used and that no one is haphazardly handling the firearm. To ensure your safety, ask the gun wrangler to show you that the weapon is empty of all bullets before you begin filming. And when on set, never point the gun directly at the actor. Instead, angle it slightly away from them. There should never be a real gun on set, and if there is, *doublecheck* there is no bullets in it. There should be someone overseeing the firearm at all times.

Sides: People constantly say "sides" in this industry. However, "sides" are just a fancy word for audition script. If you ever get instructions like "download your sides from this website" or "pick up your sides", know that these instructions are telling you what to do with your audition script.

Agent/Agencies: Agencies are companies that have agents. Agents submit talent for auditions. They receive breakdowns daily and offer whichever actor they represent who fit that role. Agents are always searching for good actors to represent. They fight to get them auditions and jobs so that they can take a percentage of their job earnings.

Agents may also legally negotiate on your contracts. Agents make about 10-20% on the money that you earn. YOU SHOULD NEVER PAY AN AGENT UPFRONT. A good agent is important, but not necessary for starting an acting career.

Manager: A manager "manages" and advises your career. They are different from an agent, although parts of their job may overlap. They collect 10-20% off of your paycheck, as well. They help move your career forward. They guide you to get better training, help get you roles, and take your career to the next level. They know you, your skill, and who you are as an actor. Their job is to help keep you working. Managers are usually harder to get than agents and prefer for you to have experience (unless they manage brand new actors.)

Managers are the people you ask for help when choosing your headshots, going to a red carpet, and improving your audition technique. They give you advice, and they help you succeed. Wendy Alane Wright is a manager, and that is why her videos on acting are so helpful to actors. Parents often manage their young kid actors. However, parents are not necessarily the best replacement for a manager.

Student Film: Student films are films made by students taking some sort of filmmaking class (usually in college)! Students are taught film etiquette in their courses, so the set is generally reasonably professional. However, the footage you might get from a student film may not be that great, because they are baby filmmakers. And often, the directors and prop masters might be entirely new to the process. You have be aware of what is happening on set at all times, because with student films you are in the hand of college students. When working on a student film, be sure to communicate your needs.

Student films may offer a small amount of exposure. Students often show their films on campus in a showcase. Also, the quality of their equipment usually is very nice, because they are using the colleges' equipment!

However, the film's quality will depend on the filmmaker's skill level.

When you audition for a student film you will probably audition on campus. And finding the building you are auditioning in can be extremely difficult sometimes! Leave extra early for student film auditions. Bring a friend with you if you are unfamiliar with the area.

Indie Film: Indie Films are a short way of saying "independent film." The general idea is that indie films are movies made independent of a film studio. Most aspiring filmmakers make indie films while keeping a day job. They raise the money themselves, gather the crew themselves, and will self-distribute or pitch the film to larger distribution companies. You may do many indie movies early on in your career.

Some indie projects can afford to pay you, but most cannot. Indie films usually have a smaller budget because they are self-financed. But, there are some big-budget indies that have made millions and done well. My favorite indie movie is produced by Luca Guagadnino, "Call Me By Your Name." It earned 41 million dollars, and it launched the career of new arrival young actor Timothee Chalamet.

However, Luca was an established director and received 3.5 million in funding to make this film. While his movie was relatively low budget movie, Luca had the experience and connections to create a hit.

You will have many different kinds of experiences on indie film sets. I have done indie projects where the creators were organized, professional, timely, and experienced. I have done indie projects where the director was lost, the crew inexperienced, and the actors were left clueless.

So what should you do if you get on an unprofessional set? If anything can harm you or your family, leave ASAP. Do not be on set alone as a minor, and if you are a young girl 18+, you may still want to have someone trustworthy on set with you. If you feel like you are being treated poorly, or being asked to compromise your morals, you can walk away. It is good to avoid burning bridges, but it much better to be safe . Respect yourself and your worth as an actor. You will always find something better.

Web Series: Web series are basically mini TV shows, distributed online, on platforms like YouTube or Vimeo. Often web series are indie projects funded by the creator or a fundraising campaign. Web Series belong under the "Internet/New Media" category on your resume. If a web series amasses a serious online viewing, it can create real opportunities for the people in them. For example *Awkward Black Girl was* a web series that created immense opportunity for its actors and creators, which eventually launched Issa Rae's career and helped land her an actor/writer/producer role in HBO's Insecure.

Copy/credit/meals: You will see this many phrase times in the description of an audition or a breakdown. It means that your compensation for being in the film is a copy of the film, credit for being in the film, and free meals! Aka, they are not paying you.

TIP: Make the creators hold to their end of the deal. Even though they are not paying you, many creators will still balk when it comes to giving you your footage. This is because of many reasons, like the project was not finished, or they lost the footage. It has happened to me! I was waiting for them to give me my copy, and they ghosted me. This can be incredibly frustrating, but do not give up. Keep asking them for your copy and credit. You deserve your footage!

Pre, production, and post: These are the different stages in the film-making process. Pre-production is the creation and planning stage of a film. Writing of the script, making a storyboard for the film shots, picking locations, the auditions, gathering the crew, organizing it all - all of this is in pre-production. Production is when the movie gets filmed. Post-production is what happens after the final shot, from the editing to cover design to the distribution. A lot of films get stuck in the post-production stage. Editing can be the longest part of the whole process, and after editing, the movie has to be marketed. Filmmakers may spend a lot of time trying to get their films in showcases and to bigger studios before sharing it publicly.

Rate: Every project has a rate. The rate is how much you will be paid for the commercial, or the film, etc. per day or week. If there is a pay rate, check if the pay includes the percentage owed to the agent. Rate also includes whether or not they are paying extra for the agent's commission. In the rate, they may also provide a stipend. A stipend is a small cost to cover your wardrobe, gas, and/or hotel costs. If a film offers to give you an "allowance," be sure to keep your receipts and bills handy for proof of purchase.

Room Tone: Onset, the director or PA will shout "room tone!" They are saying, "Everyone, be quiet!" Once everyone is quiet, the sound guy records the background noise in the house.

Also, if they yell "striking" on set, it means they are about to turn on a bright light. You want to avert your eyes.

Cover letter: A cover letter is a short personal, introduction note you write to the director/casting director/agent/manager, etc. to submit for representation or a role. Know that the cover letter is the very very very first impression that they get of you, so you want to be professional, concise, and polite. In most messages, you will give them your name, age range, and a concise summary of your acting experience.

Some websites will tell you exactly what to include in your submission, and if they do, stick to that. If you submit through Actors Access, a cover letter is not required, but you can add one or two lines in the notes section underlining any special skills you have that qualify you for the role. You can also use that space to request a self-tape. If I am submitting through email, I like to add 1 or 2 lines explaining why I am interested in the film.

Actors Access: Actor Access is a well-known casting service. It is free to sign up, upload your resume, and upload two headshots. Actors Access is a professional website, so they post legitimate casting calls and have many paying projects. The website gives you access to casting calls all over the US and Canada. Submissions do cost money $2 per submission, or $67 for a year. Even with that fee, it is probably the cheapest casting website in the business.

The competition on Actors Access can be steep. For one role, a casting director might receive hundreds of submissions. Actors who submit demo reels or slate shots have their profiles go to the top of the list. To have a competitive edge, you have to upload a demo reel or a performance clip, which costs $22 per minute of the clip. You can also upload a slate shot to your profile, which costs $5. If you only submit your resume and headshot, you will be at the very bottom of the list. That is a problem when 100-1000 people are fighting for the same role.

Backstage: Backstage is a handy magazine for actors, models, and dancers. They have hundreds of helpful articles by experts in the field. In each article you get a helpful perspective on industry matters. All of their articles are free, and they have helped me beyond belief! Backstage is also a legitimate casting service. You can sign up, upload your headshot, resume, demo reel, put in your statistics, and submit for projects in your area! It does cost to send for projects, but overall Backstage is an essential resource.

That is all, folks!! These are basic film that you need to know for this book. Any terms I did not cover can be easily googled for extra clarity. Use this chapter as a glossary, and refer back here if you are confused about something!

I

Beginning Your Acting Career

One

How I Started Acting

(me in my favorite play, Big Musical. I was Sydney Grimm, a reporter)

*W*hen I hear stories of actors who knew they wanted to act since they were four years old I get confused. When I was a kid, I wanted to be the Queen of Mars. How could these actors be so determined and insightful at four??

I, by contrast, *stumbled* into acting.I attended guitar lessons at a little music place near my old home. A woman I knew from my homeschool community was a voice teacher there, and she also ran a theater program. Every once in a while, when she saw me waiting in the lobby before guitar, she would passionately invite me to join her theater group. She was confident of my inevitable success. But I never gave her invitation much thought. Little did I know that one day she would be the woman who taught me everything I needed to know about the basics of acting.

In the summer of 2010, I joined my first actual theater production. A large local church held a free production each year, and tons and tons of kids from around my city would participate. I had friends who had done it the year before, so I decided to try it as a extracurricular for homeschooling.

In the year I joined, the show they put on had four leading speaking roles. Everyone wanted those rules, and considered the rest of the characters chopped liver. This was my first play ever, so I automatically assumed that I was going to be a background character. I did not expect much.

The day we received our songs and our script, I listened to the music on the way home in the car. My mom, who is my biggest cheerleader, immediately suggested that I should audition for one of the big roles: Brittany. She instantly felt that my personality suited Brittany. But I was surprised. Everyone in the play told me that only the kids with years of experience with the program got the big parts. How could I do it?

Despite my doubts, I trusted her, and I signed up to audition for the big roles of Sara/Brittany. Although I did not think I would get it, I practiced my lines religiously. It was my very first audition, and I was very nervous. If I was going to audition big, I was going to take my audition seriously.

On my audition day, my mom and I were so nervous and inexperienced, that we decided I should wear the most grown-up, adult black dress. I came into that children's audition, nine years old, dressed to sing for a black-tie event.

So here I was, overly dressed up, and I read the lines for Sarah, and then for Brittany, and then sang a song off-key. The lines and acting choices for Brittany were instinctively more natural for me than the ones for Sarah. After a quick audition, the two ladies told me that the casting results would be shared in two weeks.

To my surprise, those were the longest two weeks of my life. I waited for their call every day. I wanted the part of Brittany more than anything in the world. I went through EVERY type of emotion: I begged God, I prayed dutifully, I gave up hope, I dared to dream. I went to sleep obsessing over this role. Man. It felt like they would never call. But they did, and I was off the charts. I remember the moment my mom handed me the phone because they wanted to talk to me. I got Brittany!

That play was a rollercoaster for me. I learned many valuable lessons, the biggest being how to have a lead role. I got a lot of attention as a main character and I was not used to that. Some of the girls who were my friends stopped being my friend once they found out I got a lead role!!! Ugh, the politics of Hollywood.

My experience with that church launched me into the theater. I finally accepted my voice teacher's invitation and I auditioned for her theater shows. My first show with her at Mozingo was my favorite theater production to this date. It was called "Big Bad Musical" and it was a musical that had a delightful twist on well-known fairytales. I played Sydney Grimm, the narrator (taken from the Grimm Brothers). Mozingo became my theater family. The group taught me basically EVERYTHING about the basics of acting.

Our musical director was the woman who invited me to start acting. She pushed her cast to ensure every performance was terrific. When you were at Mozingo, you had to audition for every single play, no matter how long you had worked with them. These auditions terrified me, but they helped me overcome my stage fright and warm up to cold reads.

I participated in 2-3 productions every year for years. I learned who I was and what I could bring to an ensemble. I learned how to break down a script, develop a character, and take acting direction. I learned how to project my voice and enunciate for the stage.The skills I learned in the theater were imperative to my later success in film. My knowledge gave me an edge over my competitors.

In theater, you learn pay attention and remember enormous amounts of blocking. On set, an actor must hit their marks precisely so the camera can focus on them. My developed focus helped me to remember my blocking on a film set. In theater, I learned the basics of storytelling and character analysis because I was always reading, writing, and performing plays. Theater gave me a network of talented creatives, who have become my friends, supporters, and advisors. My theater experience put great credits on my resume for film auditions.

And theater people are some of the most fun people you will ever meet. I do not know where I would be without them. I left theater freshman year, because balancing school, martial arts, and film became too much. But I miss the theater to this day.

Although I stumbled into acting, it became the first thing ever I did for myself. When I started acting, I was a largely quiet, introverted person. I struggled with this negative voice in my head that told me that I am, and will always be, a failure. So I never expected to be good at acting. But in acting, I could do no wrong. I could be myself. And the more I brought my personality to a role, the more people loved it.

As I fell in love with acting, acting fell in love with me. Acting became my way to express and individualize myself. I have not been able to stop thinking about acting since the first time I stepped on stage. The more I did it, the more confident I felt. The more fun I had, the more it felt right.

Two

Where to Start Your Acting Career

(Why Every Actor Should Begin in Theater)

Every day I talk to teens and young adults who want to jump right into film and TV. Some people are just eager to start a career. Others, are approaching an acting career with an impatient and entitled mindset. They expect the journey to be comfortable and they feel entitled to the "quick fame" that they see social media stars get. My conversations with these people make me think, "ahh, this is why our generation is called whiny and spoiled."

To be an actor, you have to be patient and disciplined. You must master your craft, for years before expecting any reward. That is why every actor should start their career in acting classes and theater.

My answer to any aspiring actor is… to train. Successful actors invest time and money, building up their core acting skills before pursuing their career. Every aspiring actor should begin in theater and take acting classes. Pursuing an acting career is like being a musician or an athlete. Before you can compete or perform in these fields, you must learn and conquer the skills.

What an Acting Career Demands

On a film set, you have a lot of expectations. You have to use your own personality to create dynamic characters with wildly different backstories. To do this, you must know the script inside and out. You must portray genuine raw emotions through your movement, actions, speech, body language. You also have to be extremely aware of the camera and its position relative to you. You have to memorize and recite tons of dialogue. You will need to remember any given blocking and adjust to the director's requests. You must juggle these tasks while being connected to your partner and appearing oblivious to the camera. Your performance must seem effortless.

These are skills gained over years of training, so it rare to jump from a newbie into a successful film career. You may get lucky if you are very young or talented. But for the rest of us, *it is essential to learn how to act, and to go to places to help you learn.*

World-renowned actors agree that training is imperative for every actor. Meryl Streep, Emilia Clarke, Winston Duke, Anthony Hopkins, Michael Caine, Lupita Nyong'o, and countless other actors started in theater. Looking back, I wish I had trained more earlier on in my career. I would have benefited from as much refinement as possible. So learn from my mistakes! Enroll yourself in acting classes and theater.

More Reasons Theater & Acting Classes are ESSENTIAL

my earliest theater performances

PERFORMANCE. Small classrooms and rehearsal spaces are safe environments to learn, and grow yourself as an actor. In theater, every cast member is encouraged to give their best performances, so no matter the size of your part, you will grow. And as you rehearse, you are developing a character. You will learn subconsciously from everyone just by being in the room.

In an acting class, you learn similarly to how you learn in theater. In your acting class your teacher will also give you specific critiques for improvement. Each performance in an acting class teaches you to face

10

your nerves and block out distractions while staying in character. These experiences are invaluable.

KNOWLEDGE. Acting Teachers and Theater Directors have a wealth of film, TV, commercial, and theater experience. Many of your coaches are former or current actors themselves. They have learned from their own years of research and can give you insider advice. They will evaluate you more objectively than you can evaluate yourself.

Behind one actor is the hundreds of directors, actors, and teachers who guided their way to a brilliant performance.

CONSISTENCY. Olympians train regularly, and med school students study everyday. You need to study your craft regularly. Acting classes and theater groups require you to work on your skills steadily over time. Actors who are good one week and lazy the next, grow less than the timid inexperienced actor who consistently works hard. Acting class and theater helped me to douse my perfectionism, procrastination. I had to develop a more disciplined approach to acting for the best results.

COMPETITION. Theater is a cutthroat world, and every actor is talented. Everyone has more experience, more skills, and everyone wants a main role. Competition pushes you to improve in order to get the coveted roles. In an acting class, watching others and performing in front of them helps you grow.

When I started film acting, I was solo. I was not in any acting classes, and I enjoyed it because I had no one to compare myself too. But I think that it slowed my progress. I had no one to learn from and I got complacent quickly.

In an acting class you cannot rest on your laurels. You realize you are surrounded by students who are more talented than you, or more motivated than you, or both. You learn: *Wow... I am no the only one who wants to make it.* While competition makes you motivates you outwardly, it also forces you to look inward. You have to look at the only person who has the true ability to make it all happen. Yourself.

Frequently Asked Question (FAQ): *What is the difference between acting classes, an acting coach, and theater productions?*

Acting Coach - Acting Coaches work with you one on one. They often charge by the hour or half hour. You can bring them scripts, or they can provide a curriculum for you. They will provide you undivided attention and guidance.

Having an acting coach is like hiring a tutor or a sports coach, but for acting! I have worked with one acting coach for auditions and she is terrific. When I work with her I get really targeted advice. She also lives in LA, and is pursuing her own acting career, so she gives current business advice.

Acting Classes - In an acting class, acting instruction is given to a group. The group can vary in size, of 5-10 people, 15-25, or more. Typically a class meets once a week. It might be a specific class, like an "Audition For Film" class, or a more general class that covers different topics every week. Here are some recommended beginner actor classes:

- **IMPROV.** Helps loosen you up and get you comfortable acting. These classes are also great for commercial work.
- **AUDITION FOR FILM/TELEVISION.** Also called a "Camera Technique" or "Intro To Film Acting" class. These classes help teach you how to approach auditions and learn set etiquette.
- **SCENE STUDY.** To learn how to break down a scene and develop a character.

In most acting classes, you will be assigned scenes and monologues for homework. You have to be back next week ready to perform them. You go up in front of the class and perform. Then the teachers give you critiques to improve your acting and more your performance more believable. They will also instruct you on how to present to the camera.

At the end of a session, the acting class might have a showcase for parents or other agents and directors in the industry. The acting teachers I go to right now film and produce a monologue for all of their students every six weeks, and they upload the good acting clips to their Vimeo page.

Theater - Theater are any performances that you put on. Starting out, you can join small church productions or school plays, where they will probably let you do it for free. You can also pay to be in productions. These are fail-safe ways to get acting experiences.

In professional theater companies, it is free to audition. If you get a part they might even pay you. But it is harder to get roles in professional venues.

After you audition for a theater production, you will get assigned a character, and rehearse regularly for the performance. The best part about theater is that you will see how crucial every single person's effort is to the final version. You can grow from your classmates, and learn about how a production is put together.

FAQ: *How much do acting classes cost? How about a theater production?*

An excellent question. And the answer is: It varies. It depends on your location, the quality, the size, etc.

Acting classes in my area go from around $250 to $400 for (1-3 months) of acting classes. For their day workshops/sessions, you might pay $40-$50. Right now, I pay $225 for six weeks of acting classes. For most places in your area, it is around $150 for a month of classes and $350 a month to two months. However, that price range is for local acting classes. For the high quality high in demand well-recognized acting classes, the prices can go up to $500-$700 dollars. Acting classes are expensive.

TIP: Although acting classes are expensive, auditing is free! Most acting studios and theater groups will let you do at least one class or rehearsal for free. So audit different classes/theater groups. and make sure that the class works for you.

For me, the vibe of the class is as important as the quality of their training. When I audited my current acting class, I could tell that they truly cared about each one of their student. Do not be fooled by vague promises on their website. See their work first hand.

Acting coaches typically cost $45-$60 dollars per 30 minutes. If I work with an acting coach, I prefer to Skype with one from LA. They know the most about the actual Hollywood business, and have been trained by the best in LA.

The cost of involving yourself in theater varies. Some theater productions are free, like the ones at a church or your school. Do as MANY of those as possible if you can't afford other venues. In other places, you may have to pay to be a part of production (usually a 3-6 month commitment), and it can go from $100 - $400. It is not exciting to fork over $300 bucks for a theater production, especially because you will usually start in smaller roles, but the experience is invaluable!

Do not go for the most expensive or cheapest acting group. Find the person or place that cares the most about their students. Size is also an important factor to think about. For example, I feel overcrowded and drowned out in a big theater group. But sometimes when a place is too small, there are little chances for growth. You have to find what is right for you.

FAQ: *How can I convince my parents to let me take acting classes?*

I sympathize with any kid struggling to tell their parents their performing dreams. When I began acting, I luckily never had to endure a scary talk with my parents. My mom actually encouraged me to start theater, and my parents were generally supportive when it came to their financial support. They had some concerns, but overall, it was easy for me to get their approval.

But it is not the same for everyone. Understand that when parents hear that their kids want to pursue an entertainment career, they become concerned because they know that entertainment is an infamously ruthless industry. Earning a living by performing is hard, and the industry is even rough mentally on the people who succeed.

When you tell them, you have to be prepared. Some parents will be receptive, but only if they know that you will take it seriously and commit 100%. Research and draw up a detailed plan of how you will pursue acting. Be ready to explain to them how the industry works, how you plan to make money, and how you will move your career forward. If needed, create a spreadsheet of the money/logistics needed to invest in your career. Prepare to answer any question that they have so they can trust you.

If you think that your parents will not be receptive, you can try and get them used to this idea slowly. Instead of telling them directly, you could ask for their permission to do small, acting related things. You could ask, "Hey can I take some acting classes?", or tell them "My school is putting on a musical, and I would like to audition!"

You could give them multiple reasons for letting you enroll in an acting program. Tell them acting s a great way to build confidence, or public speaking skills, or to make friends. These are ideas that parents like to support, because they want the best for their kids. As you tell them this, you can ease them into your pursuit of acting career. As your parents see your continued success, your growth, your performances and your hustle, they could be more likely to accept this career path.

When my mom found out that I wanted to be an actor, and not just do acting, it her took a little while to adjust to the idea. She was supportive, but she wanted me to have a backup degree, in case my dreams did not work out. She told me I could not drop-out. I had to continue my school, do my other extracurriculars, and get good grades.

You may have to make similar promises. Get ready to guarantee great behavior and great grades. Assure them that you will prioritize family and school. Be smart. Negotiate. If you parents' disapproval will be an issue, do whatever you need to do to get their blessing. Good grades and good behavior are small sacrifices for doing what you love.

If your parents are firmly against you starting an acting career, that is not the end of the road. You may have to focus on developing your acting at home, until you are financially independent and you can support yourself and your career. You can always educate yourself online, even if you are not currently in acting training. Use your allowance or work a job to buy acting books. Listen to webinars. Buy online coaching. Read about the acting business and watch videos on acting.

Along with studying the business, you can practice the skill on your own. Record yourself performing monologues that you find online. Monologues are super easy to find. You can also pull them from Netflix shows, movies, or write your own! You can find acting scripts and acting technique books at the library for free. Practice with these materials, film yourself, and watch yourself. Join Facebook acting groups and respectfully ask people to critique your performances. So many resources on the internet at your disposal.

Your parents may support your career, but they may not have the money to pay for the acting classes, headshots, traveling etc. When I started film acting, my parents had just gotten divorced. Let's just say, child support was insufficient and unreliable. My family went through financial hardships, and there was a time in my acting career where I could not afford classes or coaching.

If you are in a similar situation, I truly sympathize. I encourage you to consider your options. You can continue to work on your acting career at home until you can raise money for acting classes or work a job.

You can also try to raise funds in other ways. You can trade services – offer to sweep or do other multiple chores in exchange for tutoring or enrollment in an acting class. Many established acting centers also have need-based scholarships, and you can apply for them!! You can also do your chores for your parents, neighbors, or friends to raise money. Sweeping porches, babysitting, raking leaves, mowing lawns - anything you can do to raise the money! When you get old enough, you can work a job and use that money to pay for your acting classes.

TIP: Iactingstudios.com is a website that offers a ton of helpful acting classes.

You cannot put the courses on your resume, but you can watch hours of acting teachers teaching and critiquing actors in various aspects of their craft. They have classes on everything from monologues, to commercials, to auditions, to scene analysis - you name it! Iactingstudios.com was super helpful for me as a beginning actress.

Their original prices are costly, but if you subscribe to their website, they regularly offer discounts of 60%, 75%, and even 80% off of their prices. These discounts can bring the program down to even 10 dollars per month. When my mom was low on money, I used iactingstudios.com for a few months, and it genuinely helped get me started. Masterclass.com is another website, where famous actors like Samuel L. Jackson and Natalie Portman teach acting. I have heard that website is beneficial to a lot of actors.

FAQ: *How can I find acting classes?*

Start by googling something like "acting classes in Toronto."Once you have gone through a few pages, try a slightly different keyword search. You will get some overlapping results, but you will also find some new results. Keep on searching, changing little keywords and adding to your list until you exhaust your search options.

Start being ready to spend many long hours doing research. Be willing to read books, watch videos, comb through pages. Keep a Google Doc/email open, and save the links in the Google Docs for the classes that you are interested in. Have a gigantic acting resource list to collect all of the helpful links that you will acquire in this book and later on. After a few months, you will have so many resources you will not know what to do with them. You will learn so much about your local industry, and audition hotspots. Dedicated, detailed work will pay off in the end. Google is an actor's best friend.

However, the internet will not answer everything. If you need help, you can also ask for it. You can call local theater centers and ask them for referrals on acting classes. You can email your local film office (google it) and ask them for information. If you have any actor friends, especially actor friends who book jobs regularly, ask them where they train. Join Facebook groups for your area and ask the group for suggestions.

Notice which places get mentioned often and how people talk about an acting teacher/coach/class/ theater production! If there are a couple of classes you want to join, ask forums and facebook groups for their thoughts, and look for reviews. You do not have to get through your acting career alone. Asking is a useful skill I wish I had learned a long time ago.

Three

How I Went From Stage to Film

getting ready for set

*T*he Time I Fell in Love...With A Set

My first time on set was magical. In 2014, I went on a huge, multi-camera gameshow in 2014. This gameshow launched my career. And the set of the gameshow was not just an average, everyday, indie set. The set was fancy and probably expensive. On the stage there was a podium for every competitor, and it had our *names* on them. The stage also had this huge, beautiful backdrop, with large bright lights, and big cameras that zoomed back and forth. There was a teleprompter for the host, Josh Duggar. And there was a whole audience. The Bible Bee, the hosts of the show, gave us the whole experience of an established gameshow- the lights, the camera, and the action. I had never done anything like it, and I do not know if I ever will again.

This set woke me up to what the possibilities of film and television could be. I learned that day how much I love performing and the camera. My experience was unbelievably glamorous and it definitely kinda spoiled me to any following on set experiences on set later on. The gameshow was a quality project that I would have dreamed of doing at thirty years old. And here I was doing it at age thirteen. How did I get here?

How I Got On the Gameshow

2014. I was in a competition called the Bible Bee, and I had just qualified for the Bible Bee Nationals. In the Bible Bee, thousands of kids study a book of the Bible, and memorize large amounts of scripture, and compete for cash prizes. Competitors must answer very challenging questions on the material and will be asked to recite thousands of Bible verses word perfect.

It is a very demanding competition. A word quoted wrong can mean the difference between thousands of scholarships and being eliminated. The Bible Bee has three age groups. I was in the 11-15 age group called the Juniors. The top 15 from each age group move onto semi-finals. The top five go to finals, where the first place winner wins $50,000.

There was a lot of money at stake, and with it, a crazy amount of pressure.

I spent almost every waking hour reciting verses, studying obscure Hebrew etymology, and committing large chunks of scripture to memory. The Bible Bee was a significant part of my life, and it taught me a lot about being disciplined, working smart, and doing your very best.

One day, in October or September of 2014, I was pouring over verses, and I casually checked the Bible Bee website. I saw a new page. The Bible Bee was going to hosting a Gameshow that year. A GAMESHOW!!! It was going to be a televised segment format like Jeopardy or the Spelling Bee. Instead of spelling words, contestants would be quizzed on Bible verses and trivia.

I had been doing the Bible Bee for six years, and this was the first time that something like this had EVER happened. The gameshow was beyond my wildest dreams. It combined my love for television with my love for the Bible. In my heart, I knew that this was a once in a lifetime opportunity.

Upon reading that announcement, I felt like I was going to die if I was not selected to be in the show. I checked the website every day. I obsessed over the prizes, and I dreamed of who could be my competition. I prayed every day as hard as I could for God to allow me to be in the game show.

The submission process was simple: You submit a video audition, and then you compete at Nationals. At Nationals, they would announce who got into the game show. The audition requirements were also straightforward. You were supposed to answer questions such as "what have you learned from the Bible Bee" and "what is unique about you" etc.

I transferred my obsession to my audition video. I redid it several times. I discussed a game plan with my mom, filmed it, edited it, sent it in, prayed harder, and went back to my studies. More than winning the Bible Bee, I just wanted to be on the game show. Without realizing it, my focus changed. I wanted the show more than I wanted to win.

At Nationals, I did well but not as well as I had hoped. I placed 22/100, 7 away from making the top 15. After finding my score, all I had left was to find out I had made it into the gameshow. I waited on stage with the other 100 contestants. As they were announcing the first gameshow contestants, my heart sank further and further. I thought had not made it.

The happiness when they called my name, was unparalleled. I was going to be in the FIRST ever Bible Bee Game Show episode *EVER* filmed. Guys, you do not understand how much this affected my life.

We had one or two days notice before the filming started — the best two days of my life. We used the day, my mom and I, to do what we always do before an acting event. We went shopping.

First Episode Ever of the Bible Bee Gameshow

Visualizing Success

Many people have immense amounts of luck and talent. However they can be surpassed by someone hungrier, with a better drive to make it happen. The drive comes from having a clear goal. Law of Attraction is real folks, and when I dreamed about participating in the Game Show, I was able to attract it to myself.

I paired that dream with hard work. I had the qualifications; I was a high-placing contestant in the Bible Bee who had been competing for years. But success comes with preparation meets opportunity. You need to prepare by dreaming about the possibilities. When they arrive, you have to be ready to take advantage of them. Being ready comes from doing the hard work.

I did not do as well in the Gameshow as I wanted. I would procrastinate my studying, and when I got on stage, I made careless mistakes. I let my low self esteem and fears rob me of my belief in myself. I never gave 1000% to my Bible Bee dreams, because a voice in the back of my mind told me that I was not good enough. Learn from me. Do not let self-doubt stop you from fully committing and executing your dreams, as it has for me. Dream big and believe in yourself.

BE DISCREET (Film Set Etiquette)

As soon as I found out that I was in the Game Show, I went straight to Instagram. I posted a picture, and announcing it. I tagged the company that was hosting it, and I used all the discoverable hashtags possible. Thirty minutes later, my mom got a call. They asked me to take down the post because we had signed a non-disclosure agreement. The agreement said that **NOTHING** about the television show was supposed to be shared... OOPS!! They were polite but very firm about it.

With social media, it is SO easy to overshare. But you must be discrete. Often, directors and producers often do not want any part of their project publicized. So an important rule of film set etiquette is:

Do not share anything related to the project at ALL without explicit permission!!!

Sharing without explicit permission can get you kicked off of a set or ruin your reputation. That call from the Bible Bee Headquarters was a wakeup call for me. They easily could have kicked me off for my Instagram post.

Since then, I have learned from my mistakes. As a YouTuber, I always want to vlog "behind the scenes" for every project that I am on. But now I never film a behind the scenes or post anything without talking to the director. If you are going on an audition:

- Do not take a picture of the audition room, or show the casting call publicly.
- Do not mention the role you are going for.
- Do not share the name of the film, or the company hosting the casting.
- Never share any contact information linked to a casting or a film set.

On my Instagram, if I go to an audition, photoshoot, or film set, I only say something general about the event. I only make exceptions when I have asked the director for permission to share pictures or if I am reposting what they already posted. Publicizing information is a situation where it is better to be safe than sorry.

Preparing To Go On Set

I was very nervous when I arrived at the Game Show Conference Room. My mom and brother were with me. They helped me sign in, and then we went into the preparation room. It was like a luxury communal trailer. Makeup artists and PAs ran around, and there were snacks and magazines to read. I sat in a chair while they did my makeup. *Such* a spoiler to all other on-set experiences.

The gameshow was filming before the Duggar scandals. So at one point, I looked over and realized that Josh Duggar, the C E L E B R I T Y from 19 and Counting, was sitting across from me getting his makeup done. He was the host of the show.

At this time, I and all of my friends were obsessed with his family's show.

24

We had watched him on screen for a few years!! I SCREAMED internally. I whispered to my mom, "Mommy, it is Josh Duggar!" She laughed and reminded me that he was just like any other person. Still, I was in so much awe. He eventually said hi to me and struck up a friendly conversation. I remember being super shy. Josh Duggar was super fun and cheery, and he engaged with the whole room. He talked with my mom and me until they moved us into another room.

Do You Want to Be an Actor?

They explained the gameshow again, and then, it was time for the competition. We walked onto a huge set. A little voice in my head spoke up while I was on set. It said, *I want to do this. I want to DO this.*

I remember speaking to the lady producer. They had asked me not to say that I wanted to be an actress when I grow up because it might not go over well with the Christian audience. But then, I realized, that acting was not all I wanted to do. I wanted to do everything. I wanted to be in front of a camera. I felt so at home being there, with the spotlight on me. I wanted to be on set, all the time, with lights shining and cameras swinging wildly. I wanted to boss people around. I fell in love with film acting.

My heart was full because I had the opportunity to touch the audience with the scriptures I shared. Instead of saying each verse to get it over with, I took as long as I could. I paused, and delivered the verses in an oratory way because I wanted to touch people.

And the whole time, inwardly I kept saying: *This is what I want to do. This is what I am meant to do. I am meant to be here. God wants me to share my work on screen and video and touch people. This is what God has called me to do.* It felt so right.

The reason I have stuck to this career is that I never feel happier than if I am performing on stage, or if I am writing, or if I am sitting behind a camera. That keeps me going. That is why I am writing this book, and it is why I sacrifice my summer to write scripts and plan YouTube videos. It is why I let my acting career change me, so I can overcome my doubts to become the greatest actress that I can. If you want to start an acting career, you have to decide that is what you want to do, and commit everything to do it.

When you begin an acting career, it is going to be hard. Anyone in the industry will tell you that. Your odds of being successful are comparable to being a professional football player or to touring in a ballet company. To pursue an acting career seriously, you have to be a lunatic. But ever since that moment when I stepped on set, I realized I could not pay attention to those numbers. For me, the risk is worth the reward.

If you pursue this, be sure that this is what you love to do at the moment. Ask yourself, "Will I be happy pursuing this even if I do not make a lot of money or become famous?" Do not put pressure on yourself to know the answer, but be as honest with yourself as you can.

Knowing why you are in this career will give you the strength to pursue it even when it is hard. If you are not sure, you can try it as a hobby. But be realistic. No one will hand you anything in this industry. People are too busy grabbing things for themselves. Acting is not a career where you get success with minimal work. You have to give it everything you have got.

When someone tells me that they "want to be famous," I already know that they are screwing their chance for success, because they do not understand how the industry works. Fame is not a goal in this industry. There are many many talented, hardworking kids and teens and adults in the industry. They work hard daily, and 99% will not be famous. Do not be an actor because you "want to be on Disney" or "be like Selena Gomez."

And fame is not a solution. The only thing that will make anyone fulfilled is doing what they love, with people they love, while helping others, and progressing on their spiritual journey. Fame and riches will not fill any holes in your heart.

My goal here is not to be a voice of discouragement, but to help everyone who starts this career have a realistic approach. This career will ask a lot of you. It will ask you to face your fear of failure and to sacrifice for your craft. If acting makes you happy, you must be ready for that.

TIP: Sacrifice does not mean abandoning your responsibilities like your grades or your family. But it might look like replacing Netflix with chores so you can raise money for your career. "Sacrifice" can mean giving up hanging out with your friends for an audition. Sacrifice can mean hours and hours of research. Sacrifice looks like many things, but it rarely looks like fun.

What the Gameshow Taught Me About Hollywood

Filming for the Gameshow ended in December. A little while after, Josh Duggar's scandals broke out. He was getting kicked off TV, and many in the Christian community were ridiculing him. His scandals were a blow to my perception of him. I had talked to Josh Duggar and his wife, and I had even entertained her kids. They were some of the sweetest people I ever met. And now they were being dragged through the media for the awful things that he had done.

I learned quickly that Hollywood and capitalism did not care about my potential television career. The company decided to delay the release of the Junior Division Game show episodes. Two years later, in early 2016, they sent me a copy of a DVD. There was a note with the DVD saying that they decided not to air my episodes because of Josh's scandals.

I learned the hard way that there would be more setbacks than triumphs in acting. And any victory can just as quickly be taken away or forgotten. But I learned to tell myself: setbacks can be overcome. Everything is working out for my good.I had nothing to show for my fantastic experience. I could not, and I did not want to talk to anyone about my accomplishments, because it was tainted with his scandals. Instead of feeling happy, I could only speak about the experience with shame. Eventually, I accepted it the disappointment, but it was a huge setback in my career. It is so sad to see how someone else's actions can ruin everyone else's experience.

I cannot stress how important it is to be a good person. If you ever make it to stardom, know that your life is no longer just about you. You now stand for your family, your team, and everyone you touch. No matter who

27

you are, your actions, good & bad, affect many people.

Josh Duggar's actions affected not only his family members, but also everyone he touched, down to the little black girl who appeared in an episode he hosted. He affected all the crew and the people who invested, money, time, and energy into making those episodes. His reach extended from the producers to the parents. You may not realize it, but your choices have incredible reach. Please use your power to bring happiness and joy into the world.

II

How To Get Into Movies & TV

Four

Are You Pretty Enough For This Industry?

*A*s I began to research the acting journey and follow the lives of other actors, I started reflecting. I constantly questioned myself, "Am I pretty enough to be an actress"? I had no idea. I became convinced that my looks were a problem.

Every actress that I knew was conventionally pretty, regardless of their race. So perhaps I was not pretty enough to get cast. I thought I did not reach an acceptable amount of attractiveness and this made me completely insecure. With this insecurity came self-doubt. Maybe this career was not for me. Maybe I could never achieve my dream.

I looked for something that would keep me going. Someone to tell me I was pretty or an actress who looks like me. Eventually, I found my reason to keep going. I watched a video on beauty in Hollywood. The video was honest and it explained that yes, Hollywood has a standard of beauty. What comforted me was that the YouTuber, Jenna Larson, encouraged her viewers to do what *they* wanted to do. There are no rules, she said. If you do not see anyone who looks like you on the screen, it is time for *you* to be on the screen.

I agree with that video. Now having grown up in this industry, I would like to add my two cents. No one should ever feel "too___" to start an acting career. Feelings of being too old, too ugly, too boring... I want you to put those away. You do not have to let them hold you back.

On the flip side, no one is guaranteed success and fame. And if you do not fit into Hollywood's conventions, you will have to work twice as hard to get half as far. Many actors have to work super hard to overcome their physical and mental setbacks.

For example, people told Lea Michele from Glee that she needed to get a nose job to be successful. And her story is common. But she kept her nose and worked harder Many people in this industry are told that they cannot succeed because of their exterior features. However, when they did not let the negative comments stop them, they went against all the odds, and they made it.

So, no one can decide if you are pretty enough. "Hollywood people" have a standard of "pretty enough" for Hollywood, but it is up to you to redefine the limitations. It takes an incredible amount of work, and you may go through an incredible amount of hate (look into Leslie Jones's story from SNL) but do not let this discourage you from doing what you love. I know this is cheesy, but...be the change you want to see.

33

Find people with stories that inspire you. These people can come any field. Viola Davis was an early inspiration for me. I fell in love with her when I watched her in *The Help*. After *The Help*, Viola's career took off, and she has starred in "How to Getaway with Murder," and "Fences." By being herself, Viola Davis is breaking down so many doors. She does not fit Hollywood's standard of pretty or young or thin or light-skinned. But she DID it. She freaking DID it, at a time where NO ONE ELSE was doing what she did. Right now, Viola Davis is the proud owner of an Oscar, an Emmy AND a Tony. When I started acting, her story gave me an enormous sense of comfort. As I looked into her story, I could relate to her. She WAS like ME — African America, a woman, not light skinned. She inspired me to keep going.

Another tip is to recognize the beauty in yourself. Early on in my career, I would always compare myself to my friends. I would think, "Wow, they are gorgeous. They are white, conventionally pretty, and talented. Any one of them would do better in Hollywood than me."

As I grew older, I turned to social media to feel insecure. I felt that I did not look half as good as any of the girls I followed. And this comparison did incredible amounts of damage to my self-esteem.

I needed to realize that *I* chose this career. Not my friends, not those girls on Instagram. I chose this career, and I have to do it for myself. I have to believe that I am pretty while I do it.

Realizing I was pretty meant looking at people who looked like me, like Lilly Singh, or Viola Davis, or Mindy Kaling, or Kerry Washington. I found comfort that they were brown girls and THEY ARE AMAZING. It also meant not basing my self-worth on my looks. Knowing I was pretty meant walking into a casting room and reminding myself that I could win over casting directors with my personality, humility, and my inner beauty. Finding my beauty meant finally listening to my mom when she told me that I was pretty. It means treating myself well, doing things that make me feel beautiful, and surrounding myself with good friends. On most days, it just means looking in the mirror and deciding for myself, "I am pretty."

Five

The Importance of Learning the Business

When I was younger, I would spend hours in the library reading about film and acting

My Film Career Begins

January 2015, I flung myself full force into my career. My time in the Gameshow convinced me that I was ready. I was eager to discover what was out there. I turned to YouTube and researched as much as I could on "How to be a Film Actor." I watched Sonya Esman, Jenna Larson, Wendy Alane, and Acting is Lit My Life. These channels inspired me by letting me watch their videos, listen to their advice, and watch their careers grow. They eventually inspired me to start my own YouTube channel.

My First Mentor in the Acting Business

Out of all of the YouTubers I watched, Wendy Alane Wright (aka the Hollywood Talent Manager, or WAW) provided the most pivotal and indispensable advice. WAW is a talent manager and she has coached hundreds, probably thousands, of actors. She had also worked at FOX, been a talent agent, and had a successful acting and singing career when she was younger. Now, her clients go from being virtually unknown to booking high profile shows on ABC, Nickelodeon and Disney.

The best part is, she gives free, instruction on her Youtube channel. I spent all of my time watching WAW's video every day all day for months. From her videos, I picked up secret tips and tricks that got me ahead. I now consider it to be a fact that if you want to succeed in film acting, you NEED to watch her all of her videos. Even when I rewatch her videos, I learn brand new information.

Eventually, I was fortunate enough to be able to pay for her course, "The Winner's Circle". I could then email and get Skype coaching with her. I highly recommend purchasing this course. However, I will be sharing everything I learned from her in the following chapters.

Wendy is also someone I have been able to maintain a relationship with. I even got to interview her on my channel. After meeting with her, I compiled my acting portfolio together, got an acting coach based on her recommendations, and booked my first full-length movie.

She will inspire you, be honest, encourage you, and tell you almost everything you need to know. I will always consider her a tremendous mentor and guide. I recommend her because I want you guys to succeed in the industry.

If you want to watch my amazing interview with her, click here, or search "Marie Tagbo Wendy Alane Disney Channel Interview":

https://www.youtube.com/watch?v=NvvFanRxAw8&t=3s

Doing Your Research

Acting should be called "Show and Business" instead of merely "show-busines". The "Show" is your acting craft: the performing, and auditioning. But an acting career is not all about finding auditions and being a good actor. Many talented actors also lose jobs by being flaky, ignorant, and unprofessional.

Actors should also know how to collect a portfolio, network, find auditions, and navigate their career as a professional. That is the "business" part of show business. If you are an actor, you are now a business person, no matter your age. The key to being a successful business person is to do your research.

The skill of research is an important one to develop. Throughout your acting career, you will always need to research. For example, if you have an audition, doing research on the casting directors, company and the filmmakers involved with the project is important.

Knowledge is the antidote to staying stuck in this career. This is why I encourage you to study this book, which is filled with knowledge. There are so many other books you need to read to help you career.

How to Research

In your free time, spend your time learning and staying up to date with the acting industry. Read online sources like Backstage, the Hollywood Reporter, and Variety. Read acting books, especially ones recommended by casting directors. Here are some good books to start with:

Recommended Books for Beginner Actors

- *How I Became a Teen Actor* by ME
- *From Start to Stardom* by Lisa and Rochell Goodrich
- *Audition* by Michael Shurtleff
- *How to Break Into Show Business* by Wendy Alane Wright
- *How to Get the Part Without Falling Apart* by Margie Haber
- *How to Book Acting Jobs 3.0* by Cathy Reinking
- *Breaking Into Commercials* by Terry Berland
- *How to Be A Star Right Where You Are* by Wendy Alane Wright
- *I Booked It* by Judy Kain

These books can be found anywhere, like at the library, Barnes and Nobles, Amazon, etc.

Watch interviews with casting directors and industry professionals on Youtube and Backstage.com. It is crucial to stay up to date and adapt to the industry and new information. Gain general knowledge on (but not limited to):

- How To Market Yourself as An Actor.
- How to Find Auditions.
- How to Network.
- How to Audition.
- Handling Social Media as an Actor.
- How the Casting Room Works
- Your Own Questions

Websites To Help Your Research

Here are some extra websites that I will reference in this book. They will assist your research:

https://www.backstage.com/: Backstage is an all comprehensive acting website. They have a legitimate casting service for a subscription fee. Through Backstage, I booked my first paying commercial. Backstage's best feature is that it has HUNDREDS of free articles on *everything* in the acting industry, all written by professionals. I highly suggest that you subscribe to their newsletter, and read 1-5 pieces a day, or just search for specific topics.

http://www.secretsofahollywoodtalentmanager.com: I have already raved about how much I love Wendy Alane Wright, and here is her website. I **HIGHLY RECOMMEND** reading all of her e-books, signing up for her coaching, and watching all of her videos.

http://www.actorsaccess.com: Actors Access is a casting service where you can get auditions. Through Actors Access I have auditioned for super-exclusive movies and TV shows, including a lead role in an Amazon Prime television show. You can sign up, put up your resume, and two pictures up for free!

Just remember that every breakdown service only publicizes 30% of all available auditions. And, because Actors Access is a reasonably priced professional website, casting directors on Actors Access are flooded with submissions. It is very competitive.

Local Websites: Use Google to find local production and film companies and websites in your area. If the website has a newsletter, sign up so you can stay updated.

If you live in a large city like Atlanta, Houston, Dallas, Chicago, Miami, or a city in California, you live in an area where people make a lot more films. So find those casting calls! Go back to your computer and do more research. You should also find th websites of local agencies, photographers, acting classes, managers, etc.

Facebook: If you are not allowed to have an account, ask a parent to use theirs for you. Like and follow different film studios, agencies, directors, etc. in your area. Join FB groups for actors, directors, filmmakers in your area. Joining film and acting groups for my area helped me find more casting calls and connect with others who were making films.

https://corp.castingnetworks.com/: This another legitimate casting service. Most of their castings are for east coast and LA projects, but they do have sub-sites for different regions. You will also have to pay for some of its features. However, it is essential that you get your profile on here.

IMDBpro.com: IMDBpro lets you connect an acting profile to your film projects. As your career progresses, you will definitely need to have your profile on IMDB. IMDBpro is also great for researching agencies, casting directors, actors, managers. You can go on someone's IMDB profile and get more information on industry people and businesses. It is also a paid service.

YouTube: There are so many (FREE!) resources on YouTube that can help launch your career. For example, my channel is there to show you guys my acting journey and give you free tips and guidelines. I vlog, share "how-to" videos, and interview other industry "experts" to help you guys begin your career. You can find me at youtube.com/c/marietagbo. Watch all of my videos. Spend time watching actor interviews and tips from casting directors and managers.

http://www.anthonymeindl.com/blog/: Anthony Meindl's blogs and videos are so important for the emotional approach to an acting career. His videos speak about the psychological blocks in our own lives that are creating obstacles in our acting and career. He talks about how to release the fear of others' opinions and be authentically yourself. His videos helped pick me up when I was down and gave me confidence when I had fear in my career. His videos will not only help you as an actor; they will also help you as a person.

Check out the websites and resources in the appendix for tons more helpful articles, websites, and pages!

Six

How I Booked and Filmed My First Movie

my first movie appearance, in Abitha, a short student film

I starred in my first movie in 2015, when I was fourteen. Here is how that happened…

I had just begun to do research and look for casting calls in a serious way. Within the early few days of searching for auditions, I came across a casting call that went something like:

"Looking for Teen Girls 10-16 to be a part of our Short Film about Bullying".

The film was a non-paid student film. But I was still beyond excited about the casting call. Now at the time, the website would display how many people had already submitted for that casting call. I looked and I saw that THIRTY OTHER girls had submitted before me. THIRTY. It seemed that I was way too late for the casting call.

TIP: Girls who are aspiring actors between the ages of thirteen and eighteen, have to be ready for the competition. My agent told me that yes, girls 13-18 want to work the most in the industry. However, Hollywood hires girls in that age the least. They can be hard to market to commercially. Also, most films that star a teenager tend to feature a male. So there is less work for us and more competition. Fun.

Despite the discouragingly high interest, I just felt compelled to submit. I checked the casting every day, and I read the same words over and over. But I never submitted. Finally, *a week later*, I got up the courage to ask my mom if I should submit. She said, "what the heck," and encouraged me to submit. So, I wrote my first ever movie submission email. It went like this:

On Tue, ███████████████████M, Marie
Tagbo <████████████████h> wrote:
Hello! My name is Marie Tagbo and I
would like to audition for your Short Film. I
am 13 years old and I live in ████████.
This film sounds like an exciting
opportunity to be in front of a camera and
expand my film experience. I would to
work with girls my age, alongside a crew
and a director to create a film! If you would
like to contact me, I would be most
available by email, which is
███████**mail.com** I would really
enjoy getting to be a part of your film.
Thank you so much, Marie

I hope you enjoyed the mustaches :)

I did not receive a response for five days. I died on the inside. At the end of the week, I figured that I did not get the part. I had submitted for the movie too late. But on January 5th, the casting director emailed me back. She said that if I was still interested in auditioning, I needed to send a video audition ASAP. She attached a script with one line for my character to say and she gave me a deadline.

I read my one line, edited the tape together, and sent my audition back. I did not know it, but I was very fortunate that audition was a video audition. I could have made many mistakes in an real audition. But with a self-tape, I had control over the filming. I could make mistakes and do many different takes of my slate and my performance.

TIP: Video auditions are becoming more and more common because of the recent advances in technology, so they are something I warn you to expect as you head into your acting career. We cover self-tapes in Chapter 30.

The very next day, the casting director emailed me back. She told me that she would like to offer me the part of Brianna. I GOT THE PART!!! My very first movie submission, my very first film audition – and I got the part!! I was over the moon!

That is the story of how I got my first film role. It was the luck of the draw, I guess. I do not know how it happened.

Cast and Crew Meeting (What to Expect)

Before a film begins shooting, the director may want to do a table read so the cast can meet each other, and so the director can give give overall information. I had sashayed into the room, expecting the royal treatment.

As we read through the script, I quickly realized the significance of my role. I was just one small piece of a very massive pie. My singular line went by quickly, and it seemed to be my only line. A hard blow. As the cast meeting went on, I wondered … would I ever have a role as important as the lead girl's role? She had substantial monologues and a character arc. My character was just a story prop.

I learned a valuable lesson. I learned that I was not going to jump from brand new film actor to the star of the movie. It was going to take a lot more work, sacrifice, and time before I would be able to get bigger and better roles. Although being in a movie is a fairytale, nothing about this industry is a fantasy. It is all work.

The meeting was, however, a great experience. The meeting was well organized and the script was very well-written. The movie was about a girl who was suicidal after being bullied. It starts...with the paramedics at her house. I was enticed by every page I read.

During the read through, the cinematographer would have some the actors stand how they would be standing in the scene. He then made a square box with his fingers around the actors to imagine the framing. I had never heard of anyone doing that! It was so cool.

After the read through, we did an acting ice breaker. We stood in a circle and had to talk to each other. The warm-up was a little uncomfortable for me as I was very shy back then, but it helped me warm up! I loved how well they treated the cast and cared about the script. From the cinematographer to the writer and director, they treated everyone with respect.

Being on Set (What to Expect)

When I arrived on set, I had no idea what to expect. Here is what I ran into, and here is what you can expect to encounter the first time you go on set. I also go very in depth about my on-set experiences on my YouTube channel, so be sure to check my videos out.

The term "hurry up and wait" accurately describes life on set. When I arrived set, they briefed my friends (I had brought some of my brothers' friends because they needed more boys as extras) and me on what to do. Then we waited in a separate room. And waited and waited and waited.

When it was time to film, they rushed everyone to their spots. But when we were set up, we waited some more, while they set up the camera. Between takes, we might wait thirty seconds or ten minutes before it was time to film the next take. And then just like that, we were back in the waiting area while they filmed someone else.

Come prepared! We had gone shopping the day before, and I had brought a couple of different outfit options. It was good that I had brought options because they did not like the first outfit I had. Apparently, my first outfit would have clashed with the colors on the set. So luckily, I had something else to change into. Bring extra clothing options to set!

Go to the PA. There is always a PA or an assistant director who is down to answer your questions. You can ask them about anything – food, logistics, outfit, and more. Sometimes the director is open to questions, but often they are busy filming and organizing the overall production. Try and find the PA and ask them anything you need. Also, during filming, if the director does not give you a lot of direction, that is a good thing. It means that they like what you are doing.

Come with your lines memorized. Onset, everything is so hectic that it is hard to learn on set. Come to set *memorized*. The cameras also put a lot more pressure than you expect, and even when you know the lines well, it is easy to blank. Bring a printed script with you so you can rehearse quietly if needed.

Remember your blocking. Your director will probably give you a mark to hit, or an action to do. You have to remember this, but not make it obvious. Also, a good actor remembers the continuity. Continuity means that you have to do the same actions each take on the same line, and hit your marks. You keep continuity so in editing each take looks consistent. So if your shirt is buttoned up the first take, and you unbutton it at line "apple", you better do the same thing every time.

My first time on set, I did not know that they provide food and you are free to eat it! On the set of *Abitha*, they had orange juice and donuts and refreshments. But I was too new and scared to get anything to eat. When I finally mustered the courage to get food, a lot of the food was gone. Sad!

When you go on set, even if they cannot pay you, they <u>should</u> give you food. So do not be too afraid to eat what you need! You are going to be on set a long time.

Talking to Other Actors On Set

I was sitting next to a teenage boy who had a three or four part line in the movie. I mustered up the courage to ask if he had ever been in anything before. "Yes!" he replied with enthusiasm. He then launched into his resume, as actors often do.

He told me had been in many commercials and had done modeling projects. He had an agent and an uncle somehow connected to the industry. He had even done a huge ad for Six Flags. I walked away from the conversation intimidated by a kid half my size. I thought that somehow, his experience took away from my future potential for success. However, I had no reason to doubt myself. My career ended up filled with really cool experiences.

A few hours later, onset, I had a similar disheartening conversation. There was another girl in the movie, and she was gorgeous. She was pretty, with blonde hair, big eyes, and an outgoing personality. As she talked, I got the feeling that she felt better than the rest of us *because* of her experience. She had done many pageants and won Miss Missouri or Miss America or something. She had an agent and did modeling as well. I felt intimidated by her experience, her flippant confidence, and her beauty.

I wish I knew that there was no reason to feel insecure. Most people that you meet will never be able to do something that you cannot do as well. Through my contacts and research in this industry, I have "hustled" my way into a the same opportunities. I did a huge ad for my local Super Bowl, that has been promoted on YouTube and TV for years. I have also done few modeling experiences. I have even starred in a Macy's fashion show.

If you want something, do not hold yourself back or compare yourself to others. Do your own thing, and find ways to get what you want. Follow my tips in this book, do your own work, and you will be surprised about what happens to you! Do not let *anyone* make you feel worse about where you are in your career. Everyone is on their own journey. There is enough success for everyone.

Seven

How to Get Your First Acting Role

❦

*F*AQ: *So how can I get my first acting job? What if I have no experience? How can I book an audition?*

Hollywood can be a catch-22 because no one wants to hire you if you do not have film experience, and you cannot get film experience unless someone hires you. If you do not have any film experience, get some acting training and theater experience instead. Once you pad your resume, then you submit for film auditions.

When I submitted to the short film Abitha, I had no other movie credits on my resume. But my resume was padded with other credits. I had done tons of other workshops and theater performances. My training, combined with my gameshow experience and special skills, filled my resume. So my advice is if you do not have experience on your resume, build it up by doing theater, workshops, and classes.

While you work on getting acting experience, you can also put together your acting clips. Have three to four different clips, about 30 seconds to 1 minute long. In these clips, you should be doing a monologue or short scene. You can ask a videographer to film you or film yourself.

Different clips should be in different genre. You should have a clip of you performing a comedy, and a clip of you performing a drama. If these clips are filmed with good lighting and audio, you should upload them onto your online acting profiles. Also, upload them on YouTube and Vimeo. When you are submitting for a role, send a link to the clip that most accurately fits the role.

Get your resume and headshot together. A resume is essential for the actor's portfolio. It is a single sheet of paper with your contact information, acting experience, and acting/performance training. A headshot is just as important. It is an 8x10 photo of yourself that you will submit to casting calls and bring with you to auditions. Once you have these items you can begin submitting for movie roles.

on set, filming lead part in a movie where I get tortured

Most casting calls will ask for a headshot and resume. They will say, "please submit a photo of you and a list of your work" or "please attach your headshot and resume if you have one." More on creating your resume and headshots in the following chapters.

I always submit my resume, headshot, and performance clips for auditions, even if the casting call does not ask for them. When I was younger, having my portfolio set me apart from my competition. One time I was in the waiting room of an audition. The casting notice had not specified a resume, but I had brought mine anyway. As I was waiting, I saw a boy's audition potentially get ruined. They asked for his headshot and resume. He had not brought one. He was understandably confused, and as they questioned him more, he became even more confused. At one point, they asked him, "Do you even know what you are here for?" He seemed so lost.

The young man was so confused that he did not even know what resume was, much less how to prepare for an audition. And that is why I tell you that young actors will not have their portfolio together. So being the teen actor with the headshot and resume will make people take you more seriously. Going above and beyond makes you look more professional and experienced. It helps you stand out.

Eight

Resume Basics

～◦⟋◦◦⟍◦～

T he first step to making a resume is to understand why you need a resume. So what is a resume? Your resume is your calling card. Your resume will have your name, personal information, your experience, your training, and your special skills.

You will need a headshot and resume to submit to most auditions. Casting Directors ask for your resume to have your contact information, and to see your history with acting. Your past roles indicate your qualification for future roles. For example, if you have a lot of television roles on your resume, casting directors know you can handle a bigger role on television.

Your resume also tells a casting director about your professionalism. It is a huge red flag for a casting director if they see that your resume's columns are switched around, the labeling is off, or that you are lying on your resume. Poorly done resumes show CDs that you do not understand the acting industry. To a casting director, if you cannot handle a resume, you can not handle a part. When they see something wrong with your resume, they move on to the next actor. You do not want CDs to skip over your resume. That is why it is important to do your resume correctly.

Before I tell you how to make a resume, I wanna give a disclaimer. I have taken these resume formatting steps from experts and industry professionals with long-established and respected careers. But industry experts disagree on minute details concerning resume formation all the time. So I have done my best to give you the most accurate advice, and mention some alternatives, but you may still find a lot of people disagreeing with what I have laid out here. But I did my best!

Example of An Actor's Resume

John E. Doe
Actor/Singer
AEA

123.456.7890   6'2" / 185
john.e.doe@gmail.com   Tenor

Theatre:

Les Miserables	Marius	City Theatre Company
		Dir. George Washington
West Side Story	Tony	City Theatre Company
		Dir. John Adams
Cat on a Hot Tin Roof	Brick	City Theatre Company
		Dir. Tom Jefferson
King Lear	Edmund	Such and Such University
		Dir. Jim Madison
Carousel	Billy Bigelow	Such and Such University
		Dir. Jim Munroe
The Count of Monte Cristo	Edmond Dontes	Such and Such University
		Dir. Andrew Jackson
Into the Woods	Rapunzel's Prince	Such and Such University
		Dir. Marty Van Buren
...Charlie Brown	Snoopy	Shoestring Productions
Rock Horror Picture Show	Riff Raff	Artist Theatre Association
A Midsummer Night's Dream	Oberon	Artist Theatre Association

Film:

Four Rooms	Bell Hop (Lead)	Lion's Gate Films
		Dir. Bill Harrison

Training:

Such and Such University, BFA Musical Theatre
John Tyler, Jim Polk, Zach Taylor
Artist Theatre Association Summer Intensive '09

Another Actor's Resume Example

Actress Name

Acting agency and/or manager
logo, name and contact
information.

SAG-AEA-AFTRA

FILM

SAW XII	Mathilda	Lions Gate Films
AMERICAN PIE 9	Debbie	Universal Pictures
THE NANNY	Mrs. Wells	Indie Pictures
DAY JOB	Lead	Indie Feature - Dir. Amy Stuart
ENEMY AT THE DOOR	Lead	Indie Feature - Dir. Alan Ross
48 HOURS	Lead	Indie Feature - Dir. Bernard Gibbs
BREAKDOWN	Lead	Indie Feature - Dir. Mark Dupre
THE BRIDEGROOM	Supporting	Indie Feature - Dir. Cindy Johnson
STANISLAUS	Supporting	Indie Feature - Dir. Steve Stanford
THE 9:30 TRAIN	Supporting	Indie Feature - Dir. Yann Finn
CORNUCOPIA	Supporting	Indie Feature - Dir. Lulu Figgs
DESPERATE HUSBANDS	Supporting	Indie Feature - Dir. John Smith

TELEVISION

CSI	Recurring	CBS
BONES	Guest Star	FOX
COLD CASE	Guest Star	CBS
DESPERATE HOUSEWIVES	Guest Star	ABC
TWO AND A HALF MEN	Guest Star	CBS
UNTITLED PILOT	Series Regular	CBS
WOMEN OF THE WEST	Lead	MOW - Lifetime
STRONG MEDICINE	Guest Star	Lifetime
BABYLON 5	Guest Star	TNT
STARGATE ATLANTIS	Guest Star	SciFi Channel
LOST	Co-Star	ABC
24	Co-Star	NBC
SCRUBS	Co-Star	NBC
GREY'S ANATOMY	Co-Star	ABC
DEADWOOD	Co-Star	HBO
NCIS	Co-Star	CBS
MONK	Co-Star	NBC
GENERAL HOSPITAL	Recurring	ABC

THEATER

WIT	Susie Monahan	Ahmanson Theatre

This next resume may be a more accurate representation of what your resume will look like, since you may be a beginner.

Beginner Actor's Resume Example

TIP: When creating your resume, you would do it slightly different than this example if you were submitting for a movie. If you were submitting for a film, you would put the "FILM" category above "TELEVISION".

Your Name
Unions Go Here
(123) 456-7980

Height: 5'11   **Weight:** 170   **Hair:** Black   **Eyes:** Brown

TELEVISION:

Agents of S.H.E.I.L.D	Co-Star	ABC/Dir: Big Director
Greys Anatomy	Co-Star	ABC/Dir: Big Director
Big Bang Theory	Guest Star	CBS/Dir: Big Director

FILM:

Captain America	Supporting	Marvel./Dir: Big Time Director

THEATER: (Partial list)

Rocky Horror Show	Riff-Raff	Theater Company. Location.
True West	Lee	Theater Company. Location.
Little Shop of Horrors	Seymour	Theater Company. Location

TRAINING:

Acting Teacher (Current)	Master Class	Los Angeles
Former Acting Teacher	Cold Reading	Los Angeles
Acting Workshop	Scene Study	Los Angeles
College Classes	Big Time College. Location	

SPECIAL SKILLS:

Singing (Tenor). Dialects (Australian. British. Southern). Stand-Up Comedy

TIP: Use a resume template to help you form your resume! I have listed some resume templates in the appendix.

Nine

An Actor's Guide To Creating a Resume

⸙⸙⸙

*H*ere are the step by step instructions to creating YOUR actor's resume!

Step 1: List Your Contact Information at the Top.

When you create your resume, your contact information always goes at the top. Use the templates provided for a visual example.

- **Name:** Your name goes at the very top in big letters. Make your name is clear and bold!
- **Union Status:** Beneath your name, list your union status. Your union status is any actors labor union that you are a part of. The acting unions are Screen Actors Guild (SAG), which deals with film and television performance, or Actor's Equity Association (live theatrical performance

actors). Actors who are not in a union should put Non-Union under their name.

Actors' Union 101

SAG is the Actors' Union that deals primarily with television and film actors. SAG is the union I will be focusing on, because this book talks about getting into the film and television business.

You get into SAG by booking SAG projects. Once you book two union projects, you are required to join the union and pay union fees. Being in the union means you get paid SAG rates (that is, you get paid much better than being non-union). SAG also provide actor's insurance. However, it can be tough to get hired on SAG projects when you are non-union. SAG projects tend to hire SAG actors. Also, once you are in SAG you will have to pay fees.

Once you are SAG, you are not allowed to do non-union projects, which can make it harder to find work, depending on where you live. So it is best to be Taft-Hartley-ed or SAG-Eligible. You become SAG-eligible you have done one SAG project, and are eligible to join SAG. However you can chose not to join and you can continue to audition for non-union and union projects.

You only want to join SAG when you are working consistently, and are making a steady amount of money, and you are ready to move on from non-union work. This often only happens when you move to a bigger market like LA, or Atlanta.

More details on SAG, including the official website, in the Appendix.

- **Contact Information:** On your resume, under your name and union, list your contact information. If you do not have an agent, put your email and phone number. If you have an agency, let your agent dictate how you should list your contact information. For example, my agent has me list my Casting Networks and Actors Access information instead of my number.

- There is conflicting advice about whether or you should list your height, your weight, eye color, your website, etc. Those stats are not a requirement. You only have to list your age and or date of birth if you are under 18. The most important thing is never to put your address on your resume. Listing your address is a security threat to you. A casting director will never need your address, and it can get into the hands of the wrong people. Stay safe and leave it off.

Step 2: Create Your Headers

- Under your name and contact information, create different headers for each type of project. The categories are: Film, Television, New Media/Internet, Commercials/Industrials, Training, Special Skills. List these categories in order of your primary market. Have a different resume for each kind of project you are submitting for.
- Create a header for each category in bold lettering. Include an empty space above and below each header. If you do not have experience in a particular area, omit the category from your resume entirely.
- If you are auditioning for a movie, then your primary market is Film. If you are submitting for Film, list the categories on your resume in this order:

Film
  Television
  Commercials
  Internet/NewMedia
  Theater
  Training
  Skills.

- If you are submitting for theater, create a separate resume. But put the Theater category at the top. If you are submitting for Television put your Television credits at the top.
- Make columns under each category, as shown in the examples. Most categories will have three columns. The left column is for the project name. The middle column is for the character, and the right column is the production information.
- Training and Special Skills categories are the exceptions. Training may have two columns. You list your Special Skills in line/paragraph form.

Step 3: List Your Credits

- Put the most important credits at the top. If your credits do not fit on one page, start taking the smallest roles off (unless it is the only credit you have in a certain kind of project and you are submitting for that project). So if you only have one tiny film credit, but you are submitting for a film, keep that credit on your resume.
- Put the name of the project in the left column. In middle column, list the role that you played.

How to List Your Roles for FILM:

- Do not list your character's name. It means nothing to the casting director. They want to know the significance of the role. Instead, in the middle column, put the size of the character's role. Put "LEAD" if the character was a lead.
- If your character was a secondary character, but still had lines, most casting directors ask that you put the role on your resume as a "SUPPORTING". Put "Featured" if they had a small part (~5 lines or less).

- If you are unsure what role your character was, you can check the audition breakdown or email the director.
- If your character was an extra role, even a featured extra role, LEAVE THIS OFF YOUR RESUME. You only list roles where you had to act.
- Do not use "principal" in film terminology.

TIP: I alternate between only lead and supporting titles on my resume because it makes my resume easier to read. And now, I have so many credits, that I have removed most of my "featured" roles. Do your research, and choose your way to label your roles so that your resume is consistent.

How to List Your Roles for TELEVISION:

- When listing your character's role for TV, list your credits as Series Regular, Recurring, Recurring Guest Star, Recurring CoStar or CoStar. Use no other terminology. When you book the job, you will probably get an indication of what your part is and what to put on your resume.
- On the right column, list the name of the director, production company, network or studio. If you did a student film, put the name of university. In the right column, put whatever is MOST RECOGNIZABLE. If the production company is more notable than the director, put the production company's name. If the director is more notable, list her name. When you are listing the director's name, list like "Dir: Jane Doe".

New Media: New Media is where you put internet projects and web series credits. List a webseries credit the same as you would a television credit.

Commercials: You may not want to list your commercials on you resume. For commercials, there might be commercial conflicts. A commercial conflict is when you are auditioning for a Verizon ad, and you have already done a Sprint ad. Those two companies are competing businesses and may not want to hire the same actor. Because of this, actors often chose to hide their commercial credits, so casting directors cannot discount the actor based on their previous work.

If you have commercial credits, under the "Commercial" header, write "conflicts upon request." Then create a separate resume of your Commercials and Industrials. Format these in the same way you would for a film. Have this list ready, so you can give it to them if they request it.

Training: Here, put your acting training and education. Just like the previous columns, format your training with three columns. When you list your classes, do not put the date or the cities. In the 1st column, put the name of your training/what kind of class it is.

For example, if your class was called a "Scene Study Workshop," you should put the "Scene Study Workshop" in the left column. In the middle column, put the name of the teachers. In the third column, name the school/ acting studio. Some experts say leave out the teacher's name, and only have two columns - the two columns being the class name and the studio name.

Special Skills: Here, list any specific skills that you have. For your special skills category, list in line form, not columns.

The special skills that you list will be useful when you are submitting for commercials. In commercials, they are looking less for your acting training and looking more to see if your look and special skills fit the role.

Your special skills should not be mundane things like "being able to blink fast." On your special skills, put languages you speak fluently, unique sports, dance (and what kind). If you can juggle, do martial arts, do competitive swimming, play tennis, do fencing, can do a cartwheel or a handstand, etc. - all of those things are useful to put on your resume. Be as specific as you can! For example, if you can grow a beard, tell them how fast you can grow a beard (list as: can grow a beard in three days). List how long you have trained in something, and your level of skill.

Tips for Making Your Resume

- Make sure to proofread your resume many times. Have other people read it as well! Sometimes they can catch mistakes that your brain might pass over. Wrong spelling is extremely unprofessional. You need to make sure that there are no mistakes! Check and ensure that everything is in its right category and header. Use professional fonts, as well.
- Your resume does not need to include a message to the casting director. You do not need a letter of recommendation from any teachers. Just have your acting experience and contact information.
- Play around with different sizes, to make sure that everything fits on ONE PAGE. You will need your resume to fit on one page so you can attach it to your headshot. If you run out of space, start by eliminating the smallest/most unimportant roles/training.
- "New Media" Refers to Internet Projects, Webisodes etc. So do not put them under the film category. Label them as you would TV.
- Do not lie or exaggerate!! I get comments sometimes from people who have told me that they have "starred in Disney show". What they really mean is that they auditioned for Disney, or they were an extra on a random TV show. I can tell that they are lying, and with some quick research, I *know* that they are. Casting directors will undoubtedly be able to tell if you are lying. Lying is extremely unprofessional. It is also unnecessary and it will cost you more jobs than telling the truth will.
- Do not put extra work on your resume! Casting directors need a resume to see what <u>acting</u> experience you have. When you are an extra, you do not have a character and you did not audition. When you are an extra, you stay in the background. Therefore, your extra role is not indicative of your acting chops. So unless you are an actual character, with a name, or your acting is essential to the story line, leave the role off your resume.
- Leave off performance dates! They do not need to know <u>when</u> you did a certain project.

- Do not put dividing bars or lines between categories!
- Print out your resumes, and staple/glue them to the back of your headshots. Update your resume every time you get a new role. When you update your resume, be sure to put your new resume on the back of your headshots.
- Filling up your resume takes TIME. Do not expect to fill your resume all in one day. It takes years to get any big, noticeable credits. Do not get discouraged.
- Save and send the resume as a PDF. PDF is the universal way to share files. This makes your resume easy to send and easy to download.
- Keep an online version of your resume on Google Docs. I have three resumes. One resume has every single credit and training I have ever done. My other version is my concise, most updated, presentable version. My last version has my agencies' contact information.

Check out the Appendix for more articles written by experts from Backstage, Bonnie Gillespie and more on how to make your resume.

Ten

Headshot 101

my first set of professional headshots

The Basics of Headshots

In the previous chapter, I detailed the steps to creating your resume. Although making a resume is a very specific process, it is much easier than getting your headshots. Getting a headshot takes planning, coordination, research, and money.

When an actor wants to get new headshots, it can take them months – starting from their search for a new headshot photographer, to the moment they get their final edits back. You need to be able to answer the following questions before you start getting your headshots together:

- What are headshots?
- What makes a good headshot?
- How much do they cost?

Here the answers, and everything I learned about getting a first (and second and third) set of headshots.

What Are Headshots?

A headshot is an 8 x 10 photo of your face that you submit for auditions and roles. You will also need them for your website, your business cards, your online casting profiles, and to submit for representation. They are the logo of your acting brand. In a headshot, the focus is on the actors' faces.

What Makes a Headshot Good?

On a site like Actors Access, a casting director sifts through hundreds of submissions per role. Actors Access shows them each headshot as a tiny little thumbnail. The casting director scrolls through them quickly. So you need headshots that are eye-catching and skillfully done. Skillful photographers take good headshots, but you have to be ready to shell out good money. It is an investment, but it is one that is worth it. So what are you looking for in a headshot, and headshot photographer?

A Well Done Headshot is:

- Cropped Well. You head is placed in the top third. The focus on your eyes. Click this link to see headshots cropped well:

https://zsuttonphoto.com/crop-headshot-photography-way

- A good headshot does not have a distracting background. If the environment is distracting or dull, the casting director will not focus on you. The background should not be drawing any attention.
- In good headshots, the actor is not wearing wearing distracting clothing. Wear outfits that flatter you and compliment your skin tone.
- In good headshots, you look like the best version of your natural self.

How Should A Headshot Be Taken?

A headshot should only be taken from the shoulders up. The focus should be on the actor's face. The background should be out of focus. A headshot should be a picture of you looking nice, but also being casual and natural. It should be a current representation of you on a good day. When you walk into an audition room, you should look just your headshot.

A headshot should also clearly show your "type." Your type is the kind of characters you can play. When people look at me, they immediately assume that I am smart and enthusiastic. So my acting "type" or "category" is the preppy, best friend, enthusiastic academic girl-next-door. Within 10-30 seconds of meeting me, a casting director would naturally put me in those roles based on my look and personality.

So I take my headshots so that they reflect my type. In my headshots, I have a bright yellow shirt to complete the picture of me as a bubbly, enthusiastic, happy person. In some of my headshots, I wear glasses to show more of my academic side. I have a headshot of me smiling, and a headshot of me being serious. When a casting call comes along with my description, I can submit the perfect headshot for the part.

If you can play different kinds of characters, have different types of headshots to suggest each character. If you can play a sweet innocent girl and also a nerdy person, have two kinds of headshots. In the "innocent girl" one, wear clothing to suggest the sweet innocent girl. You could wear your hair down, and have a nice smile. Then, for the nerdy character, you can wear something more studious/buttoned up. You could have a ponytail and wear your glasses.

When the casting director picks up your headshot, they should immediately be able to see you in the part you are submitting for. Little adjustments can go a long way in helping the casting director envision you for the part.

FAQ: *How Often Should I Update My Headshots?*

You should update your headshots every time you do not look like your headshots anymore. If you are a kid, you may have to update your headshots every three to six months. Kids have to change their headshots frequently because their facial features are changing so fast. They may lose a tooth, or get braces, or grow a foot taller. Every time they undergo a drastic change like this, they should get new headshots.

As a teen, ages 12-18, you should update your headshots every six months to one year, depending on how fast you are growing. Your headshots should accurately reflect who you are right now and what ages you can play.

If you can have different hair looks, your headshot should match the hair look you are going to bring into the casting office and set. If you have a drastic change in weight, you should retake your headshots. If you have a beard, you should submit headshots where you have a beard. If you alternate between a beard and going clean-shaven, you should have two sets of headshots: one with and without a beard.

The Different Kinds of Headshots

There are different kinds of headshots — the main types being commercial and theatrical. You submit your "commercial" headshots to commercials auditions. In commercial headshots, you smile and look happy. You may have different looks within your commercial headshots. You may have a sporty look, an academic look, and then the purely typical high school kid look. In all of these commercial looks, you should be happy and smiling.

You need to have a great commercial headshot for commercials because marketing your look is critical to getting the audition. Types are a large part of the casting process in commercials. In commercials, they are looking for everyday, friendly, approachable people to sell their product. They first wanna know that you look the part, and CDs may prioritize an actors' look and special skills above their acting talent. Because commercials are an ad, they have different goals than theatrical projects.

Theatrical headshots are more serious. In a theatrical headshot you want to express your ability to have depth and emotions. Below, I have inserted a picture of my commercial and theatrical headshots so you can see what they are supposed to look like.

You can see that with my commercial headshot vs. my theatrical headshot, there is a massive change in emotions. In my commercial headshot, I have a big smile. In my theatrical headshot, I have a small smile, and my eyes have

72

depth and a mix of emotions. One director said for my theatrical headshot "I would call you in for so many roles, because of how mysterious your eyes look!" I use my theatrical headshot to submit for intense, substantial roles.

Eleven

Finding Your Type

people say my type is "bubbly" and "enthusiastic", so here is a photo I think encapsulates my type

*I*n Hollywood, almost *everyone* falls into specific categories. Actors often play the same roles over and over again. When this happens, it is called being "typecast." For example, casting directors used to automatically cast plus-size actors as the "funny best friend" or "comedic relief" role. These are, unfortunately, the split-second judgements and stereotypes casting directors make when they meet you. Although the casting process is getting less biased, it is important to know that you will often be typecast. Because of this, you need to understand your type.

To understand type, think of the parts that your favorite actor typically plays. For example, Jennifer Lawrence often plays moody, broody, irritable, unpredictable leading roles. And, you guessed it, her type is "moody irritably unpredictable leading lady". Your "Type" is the category of character that you will audition for most often in your acting career. The characters that casting directors always want to cast you as — that is your type.

Your type can also change over time because of changes to your looks, and your age range. Michael Caine has had a long career, but his type has transitioned from the Cockney nerd to the wise, renowned butler or advisor.

You want your headshots to reflect your type, so casting directors immediately know what roles to bring you in for. Many famous actors got their start by being the best in their category/type. For example, Michael Caine (who is, if you can not tell, is one of my favorite actors) was typecast as "the cool nerd friend" for a long time. Finally, he broke into more profound, more significant roles.

As teens, most of the time, we will go out for roles in a high school movie or a family drama. Within those movies, there are specific roles that casting directors will look to fill. There are the "nerd/smart" characters, the "emo kids," the "bullies," and the "neighbor girl/boy next door,". There are the "preppy cheerleaders," the "popular mean girls" and the "popular nice girls." There is the "leading girl", "leading boy," the "outcast," the "bully" and the "victim".

In family dramas, there is often categories like the "annoying younger sibling," the "rebellious/stoner teenager," the "brooding damaged orphan," or the "diligent older sibling working to take care of their younger siblings." All of these are different characters/personalities/looks that they will be casting for at our age. Most likely, you will fall into one of these categories, or a mixture of different categories.

You might be thinking, "I came here to be an actor. I want to learn how to play all kinds of characters and fit into any role." This is a very understandable concern. But I suggest that you begin to at acting like a business. In every industry, to stand out, a business has to find its niche. A business's niche is the thing it offers that no one else can, or being the best at offering whatever the niche is.

Once it capitalizes on its slot, a company can then grow and expand its services by building brand recognition and trust with its customers. When a business expands on its niche, it can begin selling many different kinds of things.

The characters that you can play based on your type are your niche. To succeed in this business, you need to be the best actor in your particular niche. If you play a "rock punk girl," whenever a casting director thinks "rock punk girl," a casting director should be thinking about you. Once casting directors (and the public) recognize and love you for what you most naturally play, then you can expand into more prominent roles.

Getting good at your niche does not mean that you should limit yourself to only one kind of character! In acting class, they will often push you into different parts that you may not get to audition for. Take those opportunities to grow yourself. And as you learn and grow, so will your niche.

You should also be open to auditions that are outside of your type because you may go on some. You can also write your own movies and break out of your niche that way. But remember, you are going to book what you are the BEST at playing. Get good at what you do and then show them what you've got.

FAQ: *How Do I Find Out My Type?*

We are often not the best at deciding our own type. We know ourselves too well, and our ego can distort our sense of reality. Those close to us can give us an idea of our type, but they are often too loving to be totally objective.

There are several places to receive good feedback on your type. Wendy Alane Wright offers a service where, for $35, you can send a video of yourself to her, and she will send you back a list of all of your types. You can access this service here:

http://www.secretsofaHollywoodtalentmanager.com/typecast

I highly recommend giving her a try.

However, if purchasing that package is too expensive, you can do the same thing for yourself for free! If you have Facebook, you can join an acting group or a "Find Your Type" group. Post a 30-sec video of you talking about something you like, or explaining the plot of a movie. You can also send three natural, well-lit pictures of yourself.

Ask people in the group what characters they think you can play and what your type is. Ask them to list ten words that describe you. They will give a more honest and accurate assessment because they are strangers, and they are not familiar with your face or personality. They will look at you similar to how a casting director will look at you.

You can ask also people, strangers and friends, to fill out an anonymous Google survey. In the survey they will be asked to view your videos/pictures. Then, they can put down their first impressions of you, and any words or characters they associate with you. If you have your family and friends fill out the survey, try to separate their answers from strangers.

You can also go up to people in the street (in a nonthreatening way) and ask them to fill out a survey about you. Keep in mind that your outfit, makeup, accessories, and mood may change people's answers. Knowing this, you can even try getting a bunch of responses in one outfit, and then wear another outfit to see how people's answers change. You will learn a lot about your core type, and how it changes with different looks.

You will be surprised. A stranger's first impressions are more accurate than you think. People can get your essence from just a few sentences out of your mouth. Others may not give you the glowing reviews you want, but they will tell you more than you think possible.

I was listening to a podcast by an relatively well-known influencer. He was talking about how he joined an acting class. In this class, no one knew who he was.

In one of the exercises, he was asked to come on stage and talk a little bit. When he was done, people would raise their hands and say the words that they associate with him. The acting class did the exercise to help the actors find their type. When the guy went up, the first person who raised her hand said "Influencer". She had not known anything about him or his background. She was able to identify his career from his vibe and a few words.

FAQ: *I hate my type. Will I really only be cast in this role?*

Sometimes, it can be discouraging when you get hear your type. Agents and managers that my type was "smart, academic and hardworking.: I was told I would play the popular athlete. I was told I would not play the leading lady, but the best friend. I would play good student characters.

Wow. Those did not seem like fun characters, I thought to myself. Maybe these experts were right, and these characters were fun, but not...not leading lady fun. Who wants to hear they are going to play a side character all of their life?

But my mom had the best thing to say to me afterward.

"I wanted to let you know, that when they told you that you were not gonna play leading lady characters, that is not necessarily true. You can totally play leading lady characters. Maybe now, maybe later. But I do not want you to to be in this career thinking that you can never play the main character."

Even though at that moment, my mom's words planted hope in me. And now I know, because of my mom's words, that one day, whether it is in six months or six years, I am going to play a leading role in a movie. It may have to be a movie made by me, but I will do it.

my lead role in Five Star Pictures' short film "Guilty Wound"

Twelve

Taking Your Own Headshots

N ow you know that you need a headshot, and you have an idea of what a good headshot might look like. But good headshots can cost anywhere from $150 - 500 dollars. However, starting out in the acting industry does not necessarily require you to go and get expensive headshots. This chapter is here so you can get temporary headshots while you are working on getting professional ones.

DISCLAIMER: Taking one's own headshots isn't really recommended by anyone in this industry.

At the beginning of your acting career, you will be submitting for small, low-budget indie projects. The people who are casting and directing these projects are probably as new to filmmaking as you are to acting. So these small projects will not require you to submit perfect headshots. Especially when you are young, you can get away with having a picture taken an amateur with an excellent camera.

My first headshot was a super lousy wall picture taken from a not so flattering angle. I will NOT show the picture in this book because it was that bad. However, this headshot got me my first film role.

After Abitha, my aunt brought her nice camera, and took this headshot of me, and I used it for a long time This is the picture:

Oh Boy.

Although there were a lot of things that I would have changed about this picture; it worked for a year! It is a clear..and I guess *adorable*... picture of my face. What makes this photo alright?

The lighting is good, the focus is on me, the background is relatively non-distracting, and I wear colors that flatter my skin tone. I am smiling, and I look like myself.

These were the highest possible quality headshots I could get without an actual headshot photographer. It served me well for months until I got my first agent!

If hiring a photographer is too expensive for you right now, I encourage you, with caution, to take your own photos. Although industry experts advise taking your own pictures, you will have to have a headshot, so if this is your last possible option, do your best. Here are a few tips to get you started:

- Ask whoever has the most experience to help you out.
- Find the highest quality camera possible.
- Chose a place with good bright lighting. Outside is always a good option. You will find the best light on a day with clouds, in an area where you are not too over or underexposed.
- Find a place with a non-distracting background, like a brick wall, building corner, or trees.
- Be sure that the lighting is in front of you and behind the photographer. To control the lighting, you can shoot in front of artificial light or in front of a window, or when there are clouds. Make sure there are no shadows on your face from the photographer or the light source. You do not want the lighting above you, because it will darken the bottom half of your face. And when the lighting is behind you, your whole face becomes dark! You want the light to be coming from behind the photographer and onto your beautiful face.
- If you are shooting inside, be sure to have a clear background. Solid neutral colors work well. Most casting directors prefer gray or blue if those colors do not clash with your undertones or skin color. Be sure that there is no clutter or and little shapes in the background. For example, do not shoot in front of a kitchen or show the vent on your wall.
- Be sure to wear flattering colors. Know what colors and clothing compliment you and your skin tone and wear those! Do not wear clothing that is going to wash you out. I know yellow and peach are always good choices for whatever I am wearing. Those colors always

compliment and bring out the richness of my skin without clashing. In the following picture, I am wearing a peach shirt, because peach goes well with my skin tone:

●●○○○ Sprint 🛜   **10:40 AM**   🔵 🌙 45% ▭ 🔌

‹   **marietagbo**

 marietagbo   •••

❤   ○   ◁   ⬛

Liked by **_.kim._.23._, _queen.jax** and **69 others**

marietagbo Courtesy of Josiah Long and
@josiahlongphotography! Be sure to check out
josiahlongphotography.com for AMAZING... more

⌂   🔍   ⊞   ♡

- Do not wear anything sparkly or eye-catching, like jewelry or sequins. The clothes you wear are supposed to compliment you, not distract from you.
- Frame the picture from your shoulders up! And make sure that the photographer does not leave excessive space on either side of your face, or at the top of the photo. Your face should naturally fill the frame. Make sure the photographer shoots the headshot according to the rule of thirds.
- Look natural! It is ok to have a little lip gloss, or foundation, maybe a smudge of eyeliner, but you want to be natural.
- If you look different from your headshot, a casting director will be unhappy. Do not overly face tune or edit your photos. If you need, take the photos to an editor who can professionally edit the. Significant alterations to your photos are glaringly obvious, and a casting director will be distrustful of your submission. Make sure the look in your headshots matches your look for the audition and onset.
- In each outfit or pose in the headshots, go mentally through different emotions. Be happy, be solemn, and br everything in between. Switching between smiling and not smiling works because you want to have lots of great options for submissions. However, do not go for displays of extreme emotions. Faces of surprise, sheer goofiness, and over the top crying often do not work well as headshots.

There are some sample headshots in the Appendix so you can see what your headshots should look like!

Thirteen

Getting Professional Headshots

In the last chapter, I outlined how to take your own headshots. However, get professional headshots done as soon as possible. If you or your parents are ready to pay for professional headshots, Yay. This chapter will help you take this step in your career.

Research

Start by googling "(your city) headshot photographers" or "(your state) headshot photographer." Be sure to specifically look for "headshot photographer." Taking good headshots requires a different kind of skill set than taking a portrait photo or taking full body shot. You want a photographer who specializes in this work.

You may still have a lot of options, even if you are only looking at headshot photographers. So start to use an evaluative eye to narrow down your list. As you go through their portfolio, ask yourself:

- Do I like their work?
- Are their headshots spectacular and eye-catching?
- Do their headshots focus on the actor?

- Do people I trust recommend them?
- Does the photographer seem skilled and experienced?
- Could I be comfortable working with them?

One of the criteria that you should evaluate is communication. When I got my first professional headshots, I loved the photographer. He talked constantly. He gave me posing tips, compliments, and, most importantly, he made me feel comfortable. I had a lot of fun because of his openness, warmth, and jokes. The constant stream of reassurance from him helped me relax in front of the camera.

You may want a photographer who is good at talking. You can get a hint of someone's personality through communication with them. From the beginning, The woman who took my most recent headshots was super sweet. She involved me during the shoot. She showed me the photos and let me take my glasses on and off. She let me be myself. I could get a sense of her professionalism through her online communication. She was super helpful in emails. She was also highly recommended by many reputable sources.

Communicate with your prospective photographers via Facebook, email or phone, until you feel comfortable and know they can put you at ease. Your photos will look better because of them. If you are not happy with them along every step of the way, fire them!

You can always ask for help! Check a photographer's online reviews. In Facebook photography/filmmaker/acting groups for your area, ask the group for their opinion on the photographers you are thinking about working with. If someone's work does not fit your criteria, strike them off the list.

getting headshots done with @josiahlongphotography

Preparing For Your Headshots

Once you have chosen your photographer and set up an appointment, it is time to pick out your outfit! Buying new clothing is my favorite thing to do when preparing for a photo shoot.

You can choose to wear clothes that you already have, especially because you are already comfortable in them. Try wearing something casual, and not formal, but not *too* informal. No logos, graphics, or pictures; a solid color shirt is best. Think of what you might wear on the first day of school, or to church, or at a casual get together.

You also want to dress as your type and age range. For example, there are a some of 18-23-year-olds in my acting class. One of them is a girl, and she is three years older than me, but she looks younger than me. So, she dresses in her headshots to reflect a high school character.

My teachers encourage the 18-23 year old boys to shave their stubble and take headshots where they look 15-18 years old. My teachers remind the boys that even though they want to play Tom Cruise and Brad Pitt characters, they will probably audition for high school characters. Casting directors prefer to hire actors who are 18+ to play high school characters for legal reasons. So think about your type and dress accordingly.

Communicate clearly with your photographer about the kinds of photos you want taken. They should have a clear idea of your type and your vision.

I suggest bringing at least two pairs of clothing. Sometimes I bring three or four different outfits. An experienced photographer should be able to pick out the best clothes for the photo shoot or have a wardrobe assistant. I discourage wearing jewelry, except for maybe small earrings. You do not want anything that will distract from your face. Nothing bulky, so no scarves or hats or anything similar.

Special Marie Headshot Beauty Tips

I learned a beauty lesson years ago. I was getting headshots taken and the day before a big pimple showed up on the side of my nose. When my picture were taken, Mount Vesuvius was visible in every single picture. It could not be edited around. Never again. Now, I incorporate skincare into my day to day routine. I take *especial* care of my skin if I know I am going to be filming or taking pictures. Here are my special tips:

The night before your headshots, get copious amounts of sleep! Sleeping helps reduce under-eye. Drink lots of water that whole week, and be consistent. Drinking Dr. Pepper all week and then chugging a gallon of water the night before might actually reverse the effects. You could get bloating or puffy eyes.

If you have normal-to-dry skin, do a face mask that will not irritate you. I suggest having a daily skin car routine that involves washing your face and using moisturizing products at night (formulas work best when they are setting in while you sleep.)

Do not eat any strange foods or try any new beauty routines right before your shoot.

Cut down on sugar to reduce acne. If you want, you can brush your teeth with baking soda every day that week to get the whitest teeth possible. Drink lots of water and moisturize well on the day of your shoot.

Remember, these beauty tips apply to both guys and girls. Skincare may seem frivolous and commonplace, but acting is a business run on beauty. Do every little bit to maximize the natural youth and beauty you already have!

Tips for Photo Taking

Being photogenic comes naturally to only a few. My earliest Instagram pictures show that I was not one of the naturally photogenic photogenic. I had to W O R K to improve my modeling skills.

So here are my tips for getting better. I have learned these tips from painful trial and error. With more practice, the more natural you will be, and that is what makes a great picture.

My first tip for taking good photos is to do practice sessions with your siblings or friend or a self timer. Frame the images from the shoulders up, like you would in a headshot session. Alternate different backgrounds around your house and neighborhood. Try different faces, angles, and emotions! See what looks good, what angles work for you, and how to position yourself. You will learn a lot about your photo technique, and you will have terrific pictures for Instagram!!

My second tip is to relax while taking pictures. Release any fear of the camera or pictures. Communicate with your photographer as much as you can. Your photographer may ask you to do poses that feel unnatural, so you will be able to relax more if you have a photographer who communicates well with you. If you are not relaxed, it will show in your pictures.

My most recent photographer had a neat trick that she would have me do when she saw me getting stiff. She would ask me to breathe, smile, and say "hi!" silently to the camera. This let me move around and breathe and it brought back my natural smile. You do not even have to say "hi" out loud, even saying "hi" in your head will help you. Overall, remember to take deep breaths, and have fun.

If you want, you can allot 15-30 mins to warm up your body before your headshot session. Google "full body stretches" or "body warm-up exercises." I believe that if your body is relaxed and stretched, you will be more comfortable and natural! Your posing will feel less awkward because you will feel more in tune with your body. You can even do facial warm-ups. Warming up helps me manipulate my face in a more natural way, and my pictures come out better.

My third tip is do nothing you are uncomfortable doing. A headshot photographer will probably not ask you to remove your shirt. (A BIG red alert if they do!). But, they could choose a ridiculous outfit for you. Or they could ask you to take pictures that distract from your vision. If this happens, you can speak up about it! If you have an idea or something that you would like to shoot - ask! You are the customer, you are paying a LOT of money, you should be happy with what you get, and you should get what you want.

My fourth tip is to remember to go through a series of emotions when you do your headshots, from happy to sad, then from serious to giddy. You want a wide range of pictures to choose from when you finish your session. You will for many different kinds of characters. One breakdown might ask for a "depressed cheerleader" where you can submit your more serious headshot. Another breakdown might be a "happy nerd" where you can submit your smiling glasses headshot. Having more nuanced choices available to choose from will help you get in the audition room!

The secret is in the eyes

Taking headshots is acting! You have to believe what you are trying to portray. If you are taking a serious headshot, your eyes have to show it. Try to think of something serious or sad, and let it shine through your face. Do not force the emotion, just think about something serious.

Same idea with smiling, happy photos — think of something or someone that makes you laugh. This will create genuine emotions. Whenever the picture is awkward, or the subject is uncomfortable with the camera, you can see it on the camera. Do do not fake or push. Relax, take a few deep breaths, and imagine something happy. Use your happiness from the inside.

Choosing Your Headshot

In your photoshoot, your photographer will take hundreds of pictures. They may upload anywhere between 20-100 photos onto a private link. Then often they send you the link, and you can choose a few of the pictures for them to edit. Sometimes, you can also buy all of the raw-unedited images for an added price.

Choosing which photos you would like the photographer to edit and finalize is a highly subjective process. I suggest that you ask people you are close to and that you trust for help. Also, ask people with good knowledge of the industry.

When I was choosing my most recent headshots, I sent my favorite screenshots to my agent and my acting teachers. I also asked my mother. I asked them because they were people who could tell when I looked my best, but they could also tell which headshots were the most marketable for the industry.

Their input influenced my final choices, but in the end, it was up to my gut. I chose the pictures of myself that struck me the most. I chose the pictures that I could not look away from.

FAQ: I have got my resume and headshot. What do I do next?

So, you have your resume and headshot! Great!! You have taken your first steps into becoming an actor or actress. I am very proud of you. You have worked so hard to get to this point. The skills that you have learned are invaluable.

Once you have your final headshots, share them. Choose one headshot and set it as your profile on all of your social media websites. With your parent's permission, post your headshots to Twitter, Instagram, and Facebook. Use hashtags to market your headshots.

If you need some examples of hashtags to use, head down to my Instagram @marietagbo. Open up the description of any of my photos. You will see long lists of hashtags that you can use. Put your headshots on your casting services profiles: Backstage, Actors Access, IMDBpro, Casting Networks, Cast It Talent, Backstage, and your website if you have one.

Now, it is time to start finding auditions! You do not need to wait for the highest quality headshots, or a full resume to start looking for auditions. You can begin to audition at any time. Starting small is ok, as long as you start.

III

The Audition Process

Fourteen

Finding Auditions

me in 2016 doing audition work for my acting class, Creative Actors

*E*veryone wants to know how to find auditions. I get asked about how to find auditions all the time. You, may not be living in LA right now and because of that, it might be hard to figure out where movies and television shows are being made in your area. But you can still be an actor without living in LA. This chapter is dedicated to helping you find auditions.

Decide Where Are You Comfortable Traveling

Know where you will and will not travel, for auditions and shoots. When I began film acting, my mom and I thought we were ready to drive anywhere in a six hour radius for auditions. So I started looking for auditions anywhere in a six-hour radius.

Then, I booked a feature film in Indiana. We realized how hard it was to drive back and forth 6 hours every other week for film shoots and auditions. After that movie, we decided to only do projects in my area, unless the project was paid.

When I was sixteen, it became hard once again for me to go to auditions and films. I was doing more and more student films, but each film required a 45 min drive to the city, and my mom and I had to stay there for the duration of the film shoot. The student films were eventually throwing off mine and my mom's schedule. I had to stop doing films until I was able to drive and stay on set by myself.

As a young actor, everything you do early on in your career will probably be a team effort with your family. So make sure that you and your family are on the same page. Communicate the commitment that each audition and project requires. Know your limitations.

Camp Tough Love, was the feature film, that I filmed in Indiana, six hours away

Finding Auditions

To find auditions, you need to find your local audition websites. An audition website is a website where filmmakers and productions companies post casting calls. Most areas have a state or city website where you can check for auditions. Most of the casting calls are for low-budget, non-union, copy-credit-meal work. These are the kinds of projects you will be auditioning a lot for as a beginning actor.

Let's pretend that you live in Seattle. If I Google "Seattle Film Auditions," I find an audition website called something "Seattle Actor". If I lived in Seattle or could travel to Seattle for auditions, a website like Seattle Actor is a website I would regularly check for auditions.

If I Google "Houston Texas Film auditions," I get a website called "Short Film Texas". This is a website I would save if I were an actor in the surrounding area looking for work. If your city is too small and does not have a website that posts castings, or no available auditions, look for auditions the nearest large city.

Signing up for Actors Access is another way to find auditions. It is free, and you can adjust the website's settings, so it notifies you when a casting call comes out that fits your profile.

Sign up for Backstage. It does cost money, but it can also help you find auditions. During my first year of acting, I interacted a lot with Backstage on Twitter. In one of their Twitter Q & A, I won a one-year membership. It was pretty awesome. By using Backstage, I have gotten casting calls, my first commercial (a paid commercial), and I have auditioned for a few projects. However, often nothing for my city, specifically for my city pops up.

Sign up for Cast It Talent and Casting Networks. I am signed up through Casting Networks through my agent, and I have the free version of Cast It Talent. I have my headshots, resume, and clips uploaded on both. I get casting calls from both regularly, and industry experts heavily recommend both of these websites, especially if you live in New York City (NYC) or LA. For Cast It Talent, if you have an agent, signing up is free. However, if you are signing up by yourself, the most basic package is $25.

Joining film and acting groups on Facebook is a great way to find auditions.

I have connected with *so* many filmmakers this way. Filmmakers will often posting castings in these groups, and not post them anywhere else. Joining Facebook groups gets you inside of the network, and gives you access to casting calls you would have never known existed. Facebook acting and film groups for your area are tremendous resources that you need to tap into to get more auditions!

Check these websites and groups regularly, like every day. You do not want to miss when casting calls come in. When you see an audition, submit for it as soon as you can!.

FAQ: What Should I Do When I Find a Casting Call?

You have been scrolling on the Internet endlessly and subscribed to Actors Access and Backstage faithfully. You have stumbled across a casting call, and you think it might be for you. Maybe it looks something like this:

Looking For Kids and Teens Aged 13-16!

Friday, February 12, 2019, 1:11 PM

Pacific Time

ENCHANTED RIVER	Producer: Jane Smith
Student Film	Director: Jane Smith
Student Film School: School of the	Writer: Jane Smith
Art Institute of Atlanta	Casting Director: Zeyi Wong
NON-UNION	Start Date: May 6 - May 21st
Location: Bulwark, Alabama	Rate of Pay: No Pay.

Sample Casting Call

Or like this:

Short Film filming in Bulwark, Alabama! Non-paying, nonunion, Copy-Credit-Meal. Shoots weekends from May 6 - May 21st. Must be willing to travel on your own budget if not local.

Premise: 2 Teens must hide their secret when something goes terribly wrong with a prank.

Maize [ages 13-16]: African American or Caucasian. A happy preppy cheerleader who has a dark secret to hide. Must be able to cry on command.

Trevor [ages 14-15]: Asian, Middle Eastern, or Ethnically Ambiguous. The jokester. Maize's best friend who likes to play pranks, but one of his pranks is too dangerous. Must be able to skateboard.

Annie [ages 8-10]: African American or Caucasian. Maize's little sister.

Please submit a resume, headshot, and your location by April 9th to be considered. Auditions will be held April 12th and 13th.

So here is: How to Breakdown a Breakdown ... :)

Look through the casting call very carefully. See if the part you are considering submitting for fits your age range and type. You may have to make judgment calls. For example, if I read the casting call above, I would consider submitting for the part of Maise. However, now I typically play ages 17-22, and since the casting call said ages 13-16, I might not submit because I am a little older. It depends on how what my gut says.

I also look at the characters' descriptions carefully. Some characters require special skills. In the example above, Trevor's breakdown says that the actor "must be able to skateboard." So only people who can skateboard proficiently should submit. If a special skill is required for a role, do not submit unless you can do that skill.

Sometimes though, the casting director will write, "[Special skill] is a plus but not required." This means they prefer actors who can do the skill, but they will still consider other actors. So even if you cannot do that skill, you can still submit.

If there is a unique skill required or preferred, and you can do that skill, write a brief note in your submission detailing your ability to perform the skill. For example, if you are a skateboarder, you can write something like "Expert skateboarder. __ years of experience."

At the top or bottom of the breakdown, they will list the film details. The breakdown includes the dates for the callbacks, the film locations, general shooting dates, etc. If it says "Location: TBD" or "Dates: TBD" - that means "to be disclosed." Look over this information, and check to make sure you can make all of the audition/film days. Make sure the project is something that you would generally be able to commit to before asking to audition. Ask your parents for permission before submitting for any project.

If at any point in the breakdown, there is something you are not comfortable with doing, or thematically, think twice before submitting. You do not have to accept any role until you have read the script through and you know exactly what is required of your character.

Fifteen

How To Submit For Auditions

filming A.I.L.Y, a lead role in a sci-fi short film

ou have found an audition! So exciting. The audition location and film dates work perfectly for you. You know that you can commit to this project. You think that this role would be the perfect fit for you. But how do you submit for auditions? Here are the basics:

On a website like Actors Access, when you are ready to submit, you click on the name of the character. Choose a headshot (and video) that you would like to submit for the role. When you are submitting, be sure to provide a headshot that matches the role. If you are auditioning for a drama or a serious deep role, chose serious headshots. If you are submitting for a nerdy girl role, select your headshot with glasses. It is handy to upload as many variations of your headshots as you can, so you can have an arsenal of different looks to choose from to submit.

You should also have filmed and uploaded different monologues and performance clips onto your profiles. You should select one of these videos to submit. It highly recommended that you include videos of your acting with your submission. This bumps your profile higher on the list.

When it is time to submit, choose the appropriate headshots and clips, and write down any notes you have. Add the role to your cart and check out. On Actors Access, submissions cost $2 per submission, unless you have paid $67 for the whole year. It will also cost more if you are submitting a video or SlateShot along with your profile. Submitting on websites like Backstage or Cast it Now is similar to submitting on Actors Access.

The process can be more straightforward if you are submitting through a website or email. If you are writing an email, I suggest that you do not put the email address in the bar until you have completed the email, and you are ready to send it off. You do not want to send an incomplete email accidentally.

How to Write a Cover Letter

A cover letter is what you send to the director along with your submission to the project. Professionals ask that you keep your cover letter short, respectful, and attach all of the information requested. I prefer to only state my age range and I only give a highlight reel of my previous work. Attach your social profiles if they are professional and acting related.

An Actor's Template For Cover Letters

I have a very basic formula that I use to write 99% of my cover letters. It has been amazing. When I attach the right headshots, performance clips, and a well-done resume, I almost always get a response. I thought it would be super helpful for you guys!

Hello (Person's Name)! My name is (Name). I am a (I either say "teenage actress" or a "young actress who plays ages ___") in (city). I have done (highlight your career/experience/training fit for the role). I came across your project (film name). The concept sounds so amazing because (reason for interest in the film and why one is interested in the film).

Below I have attached the links to my YouTube channel, my resume, my headshot and my performance clips. I would love to (either " to audition for your movie." or "audition for you on ___," and request an audition date). (One other sentence about your possible commitment/contribution to the project). Thank you so much for your consideration. Have a lovely weekend, Marie

My Youtube Channel: https://www.youtube.com/c/marietagbo

My Resume: http://resumes.actorsaccess.com/marietagbo

Instagram: https://www.instagram.com/marietagbo/

Demo Reel: www.samplelink.com

Tips For Writing an Audition Cover Letter

Be Professional. Do not beg for an audition. I typically only use a cover letter if the project is on an independent website: no lousy spelling or bad grammar. On Actors Access, sometimes CDs do not care. The cover letter can show your personality, but it must be 100% professional. Be professional, fun, authentic, and educated. Totally simple, right?

Keep It Brief. No long tangents. Keep it short, simple, and sweet. But not too short. No sending emails in all lower case like: "love acting !!! would like to audition for your movie - thx Sarah." That email does not give a very good first impression. First impressions are important!

Have Your Parents or Friend Proofread It. A second set of eyes will help prevent mistakes and grammatical errors.

Always Attach Your Headshot and Resume. Even if casting directors have not asked for these, attaching them will always help you.

State Your Availability. In the email, state as clearly as you can that you are available for all of the audition and shooting dates (if this information is available). By letting them know your availability, you are indicating that you have done your research and that you are seriously interested in the project.

Highlight Your Experience. In your email, you have a chance to convey how experienced you are. Focus on your most significant credits or the credits that suggest how well equipped you are for he role. Do not highlight conflicting credits if you are submitting for commercial work. For example, if you are submitting for an ad for Sprint, you do not want to put in the email that you have done a Verizon commercial.

Casting directors and advertisers can be turned off by the fact an actor has done an ad or a competing company. They may not even check if the commercial is still airing, they may just not audition you. In your cover letter, do not get too specific about what commercials you have been in.

Inform CDs of Pertinent Skills. If you are trained in a particular skill that matches the role, let them know! For example, if an audition for a boxing movie showed up, and you have similar or exact experience, make a note in the email of your years of experience and training.

Show Your Personality. Feel free to show your personality in your greeting. Do not be too cute or hammy, but try to find a nice middle ground where you can have fun without being weird!

After you are done submitting, that is it! You have done an awesome job!!!! You took a lot of patience, effort, learning, research, and growth to get here. Now you have the wait for the audition. After your audition, your call back. After your 1st audition or 100th audition, you might get your first job. This journey has just begun, and it is already so exciting!

Sixteen

What To Expect At Film Auditions

S o you have gotten an audition! How exciting. But now more questions pop up. What can you expect when you walk into an audition room? In this chapter, we will cover the audition process step by step.

Auditions, for the most part, are terrifying, and the nerves never completely go away. But they become more fun over time. After all, every audition is a new experience. And it can be exhilarating! It is an excellent opportunity to start a new thing. So do not worry. I remember what every aspect of starting as a newbie was like, and I am here to help you! Every audition room is different, but here I will describe what you can generally expect at most auditions and some useful general tips.

FINDING THE AUDITION ROOM

First, you will arrive and locate the building. My advice is to get to the location 15-30 minutes early. It can often take 15-30 minutes to find exactly where the audition room is and sign in. Sometimes, there is a sign like "film auditions held here!" or "(film company) here." there is not always a sign, but it can be a helpful thing to keep in mind.

113

As a minor, bring a parent with you to auditions! One time I was auditioning for a music video and the audition was in this huge corporate building. After she met my mom and me, she asked me to come upstairs with her to the audition. I went alone into the building with her. I rode the elevators alone with her and went into an office alone with her to do my audition — bad, bad bad, ahaha. I did not think about the danger I was in until I was heading downstairs with her alone. I was lucky that nothing happened. Always have your parents come with you into the building. They do not have to be in the audition room, but you want them to be nearby, especially if you are a minor.

TIP: Do not go to a residential address to audition. No one hosts auditions at their house. If they do, be extremely wary. You should take someone with you, or not go at all.

THE WAITING ROOM

After finding the building, you will probably go into a waiting room. The waiting room can be dead and empty, or it can be filled with people. Sometimes there is a line of people waiting to audition, and sometimes you are the only one there. The director or the casting assistant might hand you something to sign in with, or you might need to go to the front desk to sign in. Make sure to know your shoe size, jean size, shirt size, bust size, etc. because they might ask you to write all this down.

Practicing in the waiting room of a college open call, circa 2016

As you wait in the audition room, please be polite. Be courteous to everyone, even they are the secretary or intern. Do not have phone calls in the audition room. You may want to ask your parents not to take phone calls in the room either.

Do not be loud, rude, or annoying. Other actors in the room need their mental space to prepare. If you are rude or obnoxious in the waiting room, the casting director will find out. Many times, casting directors will have someone sit in the audition room and report back the actors' behaviors. Do not act in any way that you would not want the CD to know.

In the waiting room, there may be one or two actors who are super friendly and talkative. Be polite, but do not to engage with them too much. In my experience, many of these "talkative" actors are trying to sniff out their competition. They want to evaluate you, compare your qualifications to theirs, and see if you have a good chance of getting the role. Conversations with others can distract you and the other actors in the room. You need absolute focus! Do not let them intimidate you and suck your energy. Instead of talking to them, take your time in the waiting room to breathe, focus your nerves, and speak to yourself.

Eventually, you will be called in to audition. Someone may have given you a number and then call your number, or they may just call your name. Be ready to move immediately the second they call your name. Use the bathroom *beforehand*. In the audition room, things move fast, and they may move onto the next person if you are not ready to go.

You will probably follow someone to audition room. The person you are following may be talkative and friendly. They may explain the plot of the project to you. Or they may say nothing at all. Do not take either scenario to heart.

THE AUDITION ROOM

My acting coach taught me: Never *just* enter an audition room. People judge you from the second they see you. Never enter with your head or eyes down. Enter the audition room with your shoulders up, squared, and forward. Walk with grounded steps, an open posture and your eyes bright and alert. Be confident. Do not shake the casting director's hand unless they reach out to shake your hand first. Instead, have a greeting prepared for when you walk in, like "Good Afternoon Everyone." And FAKE TILL YOU MAKE IT.

When you enter the audition room, there may be one or two people waiting to audition you. There may be five people in the room. There may be twenty people. I have had auditions where I only saw three people in the room, but there were others watching me behind a special glass window. You never know.

One time I entered a room barely larger than my bathroom. It had a camera and two people squeezed into a tiny space. Another time, I entered a large auditorium with rows of seats and twelve to twenty people, strewn all over, all looking to cast their films.

One time, I had a callback for a local Mercy Hospital commercial. In my first audition, there were only two people in the room. During my callback, there were about fifteen people strewn about the place in various positions. They were on their laptops, on the couch, behind the camera. They mainly looked bored and disinterested. The large audience threw me off, but I kept my cool as much as I could and tried to not let it get to me. Next time, I knew to expect any number of people behind that door.

99% of the time, when you enter an audition room, they will have a spot marked for you to stand on. It will look like a little X or T on the floor. That spot will put you in front of the camera. When you enter, go straight to your mark without being told unless they give you another instruction.

Once you are on your mark, they will probably ask you to slate or to introduce yourself in some way. If you are at a theater audition, they may ask you for the name of the song that you are performing. In film, they may ask the name of the monologue that you are doing (if you choose your monologue prior to the audition). If you are doing a cold read, they may introduce you to the reader. Some casting directors may give you some back story on the script before you perform, while other people like to get right into it.

WHAT IS SLATING?

Slating is a common practice in this industry. Here are some times that you may slate:

- In a film audition.
- In a commercial audition.
- In a television audition.
- For a self-tape.
- Auditioning for an agency.
- In a 5-10 second video to upload to your casting profiles, Youtube, Vimeo, Website, and social media.

So what is slating? Slating is your introduction. It is saying information on camera like your name, your age (if you are under 18), and sometimes your agency/height/city/availability.

You typically slate immediately before you perform, and so your slate is your first impression on camera. From your slate, the casting director will have made decisions on your ability to play the part. Your slate is how they will begin to evaluate your physicality, how you fit the role, your voice, and your camera presence.

When someone is asking you to slate, they might say: "slate to the camera, and then begin whenever you are ready." This means that you should slate, and then without waiting for their request, take a deep breath and head into whatever you are performing.

How To Slate

Walk on to the camera, say your name and whatever else they ask you to say. Slate as if you are talking to a friend and show them your personality! Speak from your diaphragm, clearly, use your natural voice, and enunciate.

Pay attention when they tell you what to slate, so you can get it right, but if you need to check with them, feel free to ask again. If they do not tell you what to say, I keep the slate incredibly short. "Hi. My name is Marie Tagbo, and I am reading for the role of ___."

If they say "show us your profile," that means you should turn your face sideways from the camera to the right and left to show them both sides of your face.

In a slate, stand with your feet grounded, back straight, and make eye contact with the camera. Try to feel connected to the floor and take deep breaths. Relax so you are not stiff. Do not sway side to side, bob up and down, or fidget.

In order to improve your slates, practice slating. Film yourself saying your name, age, and agency in front of a camera, webcam, or phone. Watch yourself and have others watch you, to see how you can improve your slating technique. You may find that you are swaying without realizing it or displaying other nervous habits. I found that I have this habit of talking too fast and mumbling my words during my slate. People told me this, but I only started fixing it when I started YouTube. I was editing my videos, and I could see how I was being perceived. This helped me learn to slow down. You want to catch your nervous habits before a casting director does!

FAQ: Should I Slate in Character?

I would not suggest slating entirely in character, because your slate is how they know YOU as a person. However, your slate can reflect the mood of the project. For a light, bubbly commercial, give them a happy, bubbly slate! For a drama, you can be more toned down. But you do not need to be fully in character.

Get into character after you slate. Once you slate, take a deep breath, as long as you need to. Close your eyes and relive the moments that happen to your character right before the scene starts. Take the time you need. This is YOUR audition. Once you are ready, then you can begin.

Try not to overcomplicate slating. Slating is just introducing yourself! Practice slating in different ways, with varying uptilts of the voice. You do not have to slate the same every time, and you can switch it up to see what works for you.

WHEN THE AUDITION STARTS (aka, action!)

The moment that you start performing might be terrifying for new actors, but I hope to put things in perspective for you. First, for most indie, shorts, and especially student films, the directors have little to no idea what they are doing. This project will often be their first or second movie. They will barely even know what they are looking for in an actor, and are just as afraid of actors as we are of them. Their inexperience makes them flexible and non-judgmental. And many directors have also been actors before. They will understand what it is like to be in your shoes. Lastly, even if the director has never acted, they are human too. They are not big scary wolves who are out to get you. Most people will genuinely want you to do your best! Do not worry too much about it.

Eventually, you will be asked to perform. The cue will sound something like, "We are ready when you are ready". This is your time to shine! You have practiced, you are ready, you have put in the time, and you have got this!

AFTER YOUR PERFORMANCE

After you perform, they may ask you to perform again. For the second time, the director may give you some direction and ask you to do something a different way. How you handle direction can often determine the outcome of your audition.

For my very first audition, a theater audition, after my performance they gave me new directions, and I was completely thrown off. I was singing a song, and my mom and I had choreographed large hand motions with the words. The two casting directors sweetly said, "you had that big arm stretch at the end...and you sang that last note super flat. Try *just* singing it!! WithOUT the motions." I felt super embarrassed, and I thought I had failed. But I tried it again.

I took their direction, and they were much happier with it the second time. "See, wasn't that so much better?" I ended up booking one of the leads. I learned that getting direction is <u>not a bad thing</u>. Often, when they correct you, they are trying to see how well you listen to their instructions. It means they want to work with you, they just want to see how adjustable you are. If they can fix you in the audition room, then they can adjust you on set.

I had another audition for a prominent local web series, and this audition was a cold read. This girl was being bullied, and she gets angry, and then this cute boy comes to her rescue. I performed the script the first time, and the director gave me the impression that he liked my performance.

"That was good," he said, "Why do not we try it this time, but this time, I want you to do it a little angrier." He explained to me my backstory for being angry to get me to that emotional state. It seemed easy enough. I started rereading it. He stopped me, and again, he gave me some more direction and more explanation. He seemed to be growing a little more exasperated.

On the third read-through, I thought I was nailing it. But when I finished, I could feel by his response that I had not gotten the part. He ended the audition with a "thank you" and explained when he would let me know. There are a million reasons why I did not get the part, but *I* suspect that it was because I was not adjusting to the director's instructions.

It is imperative to be receptive to direction in the audition room. You need to be flexible enough with your acting approach to adjust your interpretation and performance to the casting director's requests. So if the casting director asks you to go to an emotional place that you had not prepared for, take a few extra seconds to get ready.

Taking acting classes and coaching will improve your ability to take criticism and redirection, because you will receive a lot of instruction. But the most important things to remember are: Do not argue, do not defend your choices, and do not be embarrassed! Just apply their advice as best as you can.

The casting director may ask you to read the other character's lines, read a new script, or say another monologue. Be prepared and always have 2-3 other monologues memorized and ready to perform at any audition. If they ask you to read for another character, be enthusiastic about it! If they hand you a new script, they may ask or give you a few moments to look over it. If you need the time, say yes! If they do not offer you that extra time, you can still ask for a few additional minutes to read over it. They may decide to send you back out and give you a chance to read over it, and then bring you back in. And if they hand you a new script, you are doing a cold read, so they will not expect you to be perfect. Just commit to whatever is on the page.

At the end of your audition, they may say "Thank you" andadd a "We will let you know at the end of ____." Do not bow, just smile, and say thank you, no matter what happened in the audition room. Leave as confidently as you came in. I always say brightly, "Have a good day everyone!" to fill up the silence after an audition. Leave head up, shoulders back, eyes bright and forward, and take big confident steps.

AND THEN LOOK!!! YOU DID IT!!! YOU JUST AUDITIONED. High five yourself, internally or externally! Be grateful for the opportunity, and be proud of yourself no matter how it went. With an audition, you can not lose. Each mistake you made is a GREAT learning opportunity. Each thing you did well is a win for you.

Leave the audition room in the audition room. If you start to overthink your auditions, you are hurting your future self. You will be less resilient with rejections if you are beating yourself up for a "bad" choice you made. When you are in the audition room, give it everything you got, and when you leave, leave it there. You need this mindset to be resilient in the acting business. Your resilience is what you need to have a successful career.

sitting at a student film audition, taking a selfie

Seventeen

The Differences Between Film and Theater

⚜

*T*heater and film auditions are very different from each other. They are wildly different mediums and you need a different style of acting to be successful in each. In this chapter, I outline the main differences between theater and film auditions, so you can know what to expect and how to prepare yourself.

Film vs. Theater

Preparation

In theater, you may be asked to dance or sing. You might have to practice a music piece, and be trained in some form of dance (especially for musical theater). Read over the audition notice carefully, because it will probably specify what you need to wear and bring for the audition. If you have questions about the audition that were not answered in the notice, you can email the casting director or the director.

In Film, Commercial, TV, & Agency Auditions (and in this chapter I will just call these "film auditions") you will probably not be asked to dance or sing. Instead, in film auditions, you might be asked to do a cold read, do improv, memorize a script given beforehand, or bring in a monologue/commercial of a certain specified length.

In both kinds of auditions, you may be asked to perform monologues, do cold reads or both.

Stage vs. Camera

In theater, there are rarely cameras to perform in front of. You will almost always be standing on a sort of stage, so the casting directors can see your stage presence. In film, there is almost always a camera in the room, and so you will be performing for the camera, and not broadly to the auditorium.

What You Perform

In theater, you will probably audition for something performed before. Many times you will be familiar with the show, because it is well-known like *Beauty and the Beast* or *Annie*. And even if you are not familiar with the show, you can probably scour the Internet and Youtube for information about the show and past performances.

In film auditions, you are almost always auditioning for an original project, with new material.

Slating

Slating may be slightly different for theater and film auditions. But for both kinds of auditions, they will instruct you on what to say and do.

Performance

There is a fundamental difference between acting for film and acting for theater. In theater, you have to speak to a whole room, as if you are in a crowded bar. You use real emotions, broad body language, and you emphasize facial expressions and diction.

The way you perform for theater is too broad for film. Film is an intimate art. The camera is right in your face, and the microphone captures everything in your voice and facial expressions. In film, you should talk as if you are speaking to a friend who is right next to you. In film, you have the same emotions and energy as theater but you use your natural voice and express more subtly.

The transition between film and theater can be difficult. It was hard for me (and many others I know) to transition from theater to film. When you have done theater for so long, you are used to being broad and showing emotions externally. Those of us who transition are continually told to quiet our voices, be less broad, stop moving around as much, and soften our facial expressions.

Casting Directors I auditioned for could tell that I had trained in theater. I tended to kind of shout at the camera. They would remind me gently, "The camera picks up everything. You do not have to be loud or project." I would realize that I had been performing for the whole room, and not for a small frame. I had not developed camera technique. Film and commercial classes are so essential to avoid these errors.

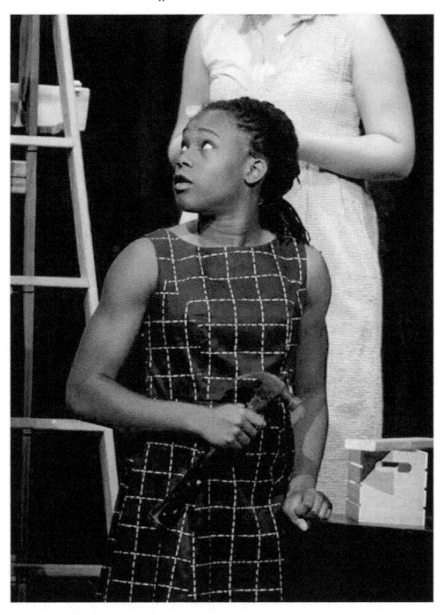

Performance Picture one of my last theater shows, Golly Gee Whiz

Eighteen

What to Wear to Auditions

~~~

*D*eciding what to wear to each audition can be my favorite part of the entire casting process. However, it often takes me hours to figure out my outfit. This is not because I am a stereotypical vain millennial female. It is because I make sure that I am dressing appropriately for each audition and character. There are few hard and fast rules for audition attire. Some casting directors care little about what you wear, while others might be turned off by your earrings. Here are a few guidelines to keep yourself and your outfit choices in the running for the part.

Dress to Suggest the Character.

If you are auditioning for a police officer, do not show up in a policeman suit bought from Party City. However, you should wear something that suggests a police officer. If you are auditioning for a police officer, you may want to wear a blue top and black pants.

If you are going out for the part of a cheerleader, you may want to wear cute preppy clothing, like a cute blouse and an appropriate skirt. In other words, if you are auditioning for a cheerleader, wear what a cheerleader would wear when she is not in uniform. If you are going for the part of an athlete, you could pull your hair back, wear sneakers, and perhaps a short-sleeved t-shirt.

If your character is rebellious, you could bring in a leather jacket over a white shirt and jeans. Dress to help the casting director see you in the role. But do not weigh yourself down with unnecessary props and Halloween costumes. Never bring props to auditions either. Or pets.

Do Your Research.

Look up the director, casting director, and production company and see what the actors, similar to your type, wore in the director's previous projects. This can help inform your clothing choices.

You can also find out what kinds of clothes and styles did actors for similar commercials/roles wear and dress to fit that. If you are auditioning for a commercial, and you know the company's name, look at their previous ads. See what clothes and colors the kids & teens your age wore in their previous commercials. Find the outfits with a color palette that match what those actors wore.

For example, If you have a Kit Kat audition, you might search for "Kit Kat Commercial" and find this video:
https://www.youtube.com/watch?v=bXUHM4RU4oU
After watching the video, you might notice that the women aged 25+ were wearing business/business casual. If you were auditioning for the role of a woman 25+ in a Kit Kat commercial then you should bring in similar business/business casual outfits to the audition.

If there is only limited information about the company's projects find similar projects. If you are auditioning for Air Heads, you can look up an ad for Sour Gummies, and see what the kids and teens your age are wearing. You can use their outfits as inspiration for what to wear to an Air Heads commercial.

You can research your outfit for any movie or TV show audition. If you are auditioning for a TV show, watch the previous episodes and see what the kids wore. For example, in Riverdale, the characters typically wear dark, cute, edgy clothing that fits a specific color scheme. If you were auditioning for Riverdale, wear clothing similar to the outfits in the show. So you would wear an outfit that is dark and edgy.

Wear Clothes That Flatter You.

Wear colors that make your eyes and skin POP, and that flatter your body shape!! Research on what looks good on your body shape and with your undertones. For me, yellow and peach are the best colors; they flatter me, and they rarely blend in with the CD's backdrop. Often CDs have a black, white, grey or blue backdrop. You may want to avoid wearing those colors.

Solid colors are almost always the best choice. Avoid clothing with a lot of sequins or sparkles or strings or slogans. Be sure to stay away from stripes, primarily black and white stripes, because they show up super awkwardly on camera!! Do not wear colors that wash you out or look flesh-colored. Wear what compliments your skin. If people always tell you that...I don't know... *purple,* brings out your skin, wear that!

Audition selfie. I am of course, wearing peach

Wear Clothes That Look and Smell Nice.

131

Make sure your clothing is not raggedy, and that it has no rips, no tears, no stains, and no smells. Iron your clothes if needed. Your outfit does not have to be brand new, but it should not look slept in or homeless.

Do Not Too Nice.

Your clothes should look nice, but this is not prom or a modeling photo session. Casting directors are looking to young actors in their real, natural look. I just got an audition request for a huge Amazon show, and the casting director specifically asked for the actors to come in natural hair and no makeup. Whenever I go to a film set with a makeup artist, they never give me much makeup.

Those in the industry prefer to keep the natural, everyday school look for young actors. If you are 11, do not come with your face fully contoured and a body-tight dress. Dress like an 11-year-old! Even if you are older, and it is more common for you to wear makeup to work or dates, keep the makeup to a minimum. CDs prefer a natural makeup look over the full-glam beauty guru makeup trend.

Ask For Help!

If you are stumped on outfit choices, ask your agent or industry expert your trust. You can also film yourself wearing the outfit and see if it looks good on camera.

Pay attention to the audition notice. Sometimes they will have suggestions on what to wear. There may be keywords like "nice casual clothing" or "suit and tie." Even the character breakdown can give you some clues. If the character is described as a "skinny boy with asthma," that can give you ideas. To play up the stereotype, you could put on a button-up shirt and khakis.

Miscellaneous Tips for Audition Outfits

- Leave some parts of the character to the imagination! Dress to suggest but let the casting director view you in the role.
- For drama, experts suggest that you should wear darker, more earth tone colors. For comedy, wear brighter, more cheery colors.
- For callbacks, wear the same outfit that you wore to the first audition. They liked the first audition, and wearing the same outfit will remind them of what they liked about your first performance.
- During your daily life, take notes on how people your age dress on television and in movies. It may be a little fancier than what they are looking for in auditions, but it will give you a good sense of what is appropriate for the casting room.
- In a self tape, wear a color that contrasts your wall. If you are using a white wall, do not wear a white shirt.

Nineteen

What to Bring to an Audition (A Checklist)

꧁

*L*ists keep me from going insane. Auditions used to make me nuts–there is *so much* to keep track of! I would always be so scared that I had forgotten something. So finally...I made a list. This audition checklist has saved my life. After using this list, I am always ready for auditions. I have never forgotten anything important for an audition. This list has helped me, and so I am so excited to include it here for you.

The first part of the checklist are the items that you MUST bring to an audition. The second part has slightly more optional items. The last part is the Do NOT bring section.

An Ultimate Audition Checklist

MUST HAVES

- HEADSHOT and RESUME. You *need* your headshot for the CD to remember who you are. Attach your resume to the back of your headshot, so that the CD can flip your headshot over and easily see your resume. You NEED a resume, even if it only has a few credits because your resume has your contact information and your experience.
- WATER. You may want to keep water in a purse, or man bag, or with your guardian, but you want to bring water. Nerves may dry out your throat, and you may be doing a lot of talking, so keep your throat moist and hydrated! Just keep water items outside the actual audition room.
- MAKEUP/ACCESSORIES. I have my makeup essentials, so I can touch up my makeup in case something goes wrong and gets smeared. Include but are not limited to: ponytails, foundation, lip gloss, earrings, hairbrushes, hair gel, mirror, face/wet wipes, and deodorant, etc.
- A PARENT. You must have a parent with you if you are under 18.
- YOUR SIDES. If they send you your script ahead of time, be sure to have it on your phone. You can also print it out.

PRETTY IMPORTANT

- EXTRA COPIES OF YOUR HEADSHOTS, RESUMES (AND SCRIPT). Something may happen to your original copies, like coffee spills, or the wind. You do not want to hand a CD a beaten up headshot and resume. Print at least five copies of your headshot and resume and keep them nearby, in the car, or maybe with your parents.
- YOUR INFORMATION. When you sign in, they may ask you for statistics about yourself that you have not checked in a while. Measure

136

yourself periodically. Have a list on your phone or car of your pant size, waist size, bust size, height, weight, hair length, hair color, shoe size, parents number and email, your number, and email. They may ask you for all of this information!

- DIRECTIONS. In case Google Maps fail, I highly recommend printing directions out! Sometimes the audition email will have added directions on how to find the audition building and parking. Be sure to print these extra instructions out as well!

TIP: You can use the app Waze to help you calculate what time you need to leave for your audition. Waze tells you about traffic, police, and lets you upload your Spotify playlists to the app. I suggest calculating using Waze and leaving 15 - 30 minutes earlier than you need to get there because you might get lost or run into traffic.

- EXTRA CLOTHES. If you are like me, you can be a little clumsy. My life is foundation stains and mysteriously scuffed shoes. Bring an extra pair of audition suitable clothing. You may even just want to have an extra outfit in your car at all times.

SOME MAYBES AND SUGGESTIONS

- DANCE SHOES (and other dance items)! You may need these for theater auditions. The audition notices may ask you to bring "jazz shoes" or "ballet shoes." You can find these at a local dance store.
- A BOOK. In the waiting room, sometimes I am too stressed to practice my script. So instead, I like to bring a book to read over. Also, some people have warned me that some casting directors look down on actors who practice their script in the audition room, if you got your script

early. Practicing your script can make you look not ready. You can always go over the script on your phone, but having a book gives you a helpful alternative.

- A VOCAL WARM UP. Doing a vocal warm-up in the car has immensely benefited my auditions. I highly suggest doing a light stretch of your voice, face, and body before auditions.
- SHEET MUSIC. If you are auditioning for musical theater, you will need sheet music to give to the pianist.
- COPY OF YOUR MONOLOGUE. If you are being asked to bring in a monologue, you might want to bring a copy of the monologue so you can practice in the car or audition room.

LEAVE THIS AT HOME

- A HUGE PURSE. You do not want to have to lug something huge and obnoxious, to and from the audition room. Unless your big bag stays with your guardian, and outside the audition room, it is better to leave it at home.
- A FRIEND. The waiting room typically has limited space, and the noise of a group could be very distracting and off-putting. As much as you might appreciate the support of people you know, auditions are not the time to bring friends/pets/or loud family members. The waiting room is for you to focus on your audition, not focus on your friend. Have them wait until afterwards to hang with you.
- A BAD ATTITUDE. If you have a bad attitude, then you really need to leave it at home. I understand that you might want the role, or be wracked with nerves, or be having a bad day, but always be kind to others. Life is always working itself out for your best. Bring your positivity, your confidence, and your gratitude. Thank God for this audition!

Twenty

Preparing For Auditions

*C*ongratulations! You submitted for a part, and the director asked you to come back on a specific date, bringing a particular set of material and read for a specific role, or say a monologue. How exciting! After a certain number of days, you will enter a room full of people, who will expect you to be fully prepared and perform. These people are judging you, to see if you are right for their project. How do you get ready for this moment?

You must now undertake the long process of preparing for this audition. Preparing for auditions is 95% of the audition. It used to take me a long time because I was trying to remember every little thing. However, it becomes more of a routine with more experience, like driving. There are some important things to do before you enter the audition room. Here are some guidelines on preparing for your audition.

Do Your Research

For every audition, I like to orient myself by doing as much research as I can on anything related to the company and the creators. My goal is to know who everything about who I am auditioning for:

- What genres of projects does this team typically cast for?
- Can I find out how they run their casting process?
- What kinds of stories does the writer like to tell?
- What is the style of the script?
- What filmmaking style does the director have?

An important question I ask is:

- What is the tone of the projects that this company has previously put out?

Most companies have a tone or genre of projects they work on. For example, Netflix originals typically have a tinge of being socially conscious and diverse. HBO shows are often edgy, racy, and dark. Amazon likes to do a lot of "period" shows.

The style and preferences of a show, its creators, and its production team are essential pieces of information that every actor must be aware of. The first step in audition prep is researching anyone mentioned as a part of the production team.

How do you find out information? Google the company! Watch old projects on their website. Find everyone in the team on IMDBpro and LinkedIn. Take notes. You will often find unexpected but helpful information.

For example, by looking at the CD's credits, you might learn that the casting director for this project was the writer for another project you submitted for. Or you may find that the company is known for its diverse casting. You do not know what you will find, but the gems you do discover by doing your research are priceless.

Learn About the Story and Project

After you are done google-stalking the production company, learn more about the project and the story.

For theater projects, you can find a lot about the project online. You can often find performances, and even the script online. You can learn information that will help you choose your audition songs and monologues.

142

For example, if I were auditioning for Beauty and the Beast, I would read the play, watch the movie, and watch performances online. Then I would try to choose a monologue that fits the character I am auditioning for, the tone of the show, and the length of what the casting office asks for, etc.

In movies, commercials, and TV, the script is often new. You may not know the whole story, or who all the characters are. It can be hard to figure out what is going on. However, there are ways to figure out more about the story.

For example, the breakdown might have a different script attached for each character. Read the other character's scripts to piece together the whole story and give yourself context. As you read the breakdown, character descriptions, and script, ask yourself:

- What can I learn about the story line?
- What sort of story does the author intend to tell?
- What is the mood? Is upbeat and comedic? Is it weird and melodramatic?
- If I were directing the script, what would each scene look like?

If a casting call ever says "based on_____," research where the project comes from.

Recently submitted for a casting call based on someone's real life. While I waited for them to call me in, I spent four hours watching any documentary and interview that I could find. I looked up the project on Wikipedia and tried to find out as much as I could on the people doing the casting. From the real person's interviews, I wrote down pages and pages of the person's history and personality. If I had been called in to audition, I would have had a depth of knowledge about the character that a lot of other actors might not have had. This research could have set me apart.

Another time a director offered me a role in my first martial art film. I was replacing a girl who had dropped out. The film came from a web series that the guy had done. His web series had about thirty episodes out on YouTube, so I watched at least fifteen of them. I got a general sense of the director's skill. I also learned the storyline, the style of acting, and what sort of martial art moves the director likes to use in his filming. My research helped me connect to the director, understand the script a lot better, and get into character. The director was impressed with me because his lead had had no idea how to handle the choreography and did not understand the general storyline of the film. He appreciated not having to explain the storyline to me. Do your research, guys!

RECAP: The first step in audition preparation is to research the company's previous film/theater projects to understand more about the company, their style, and what they do. Find out as much about the project by reading related materials.

Gather Your Supplies.

From my experience, you should start prepping your materials and supplies *a week ahead of time*. Your audition supplies are things like your audition outfit, resume, headshot, dance routine, audition song, and your monologue.

Your current closet may not have an audition ready outfit, so you will want to plan what you are going to wear and buy any missing items.

You will also need a headshot that is updated and printed. For same day printing, you can order headshots at your local Walgreens for 4.99 per photo. If you Google "photo coupons for Walgreens," you can often find discounts. However, to be on the safe side, have your headshot printed out at least a day before it is needed.

You will also want to make sure your resume has your updated credits and contact information. Check for spelling errors and correctly organized credits. Then, you want to staple your headshot to the back of your resume. You do not want to wait till the night before to get your headshot and resume in case your printer breaks down, or Walgreens closes earlier than you expected. You may also want to print out extra copies. I typically have about five copies of my headshot and resume stapled together in a little folder at all times.

Prepare Your Performance Material

For a theater audition, you may need to prepare an audition song. I will give brief tips on preparing songs for auditions, because theater is not the focus of this book. But here is what I learned from theater:

To prepare a song, first choose an appropriate song for the audition. Work your song over with a vocal teacher, memorize it, and practice it daily! Buy your sheet music in the right key, practice the song in that key, and bring the sheet music to the audition. For musical theater auditions, I would practice my music five to six a day, starting at least two weeks before the audition. Professional theater actors work on their songs for longer. You must be comfortable enough with the song that you nail your performance. My martial arts instructor says this gem: - "We do not practice so we can get it right, we practice so that we never get it wrong."

There are so many other amazing books and articles you can find. They will give you so way more amazing instructions on theater auditions than I will. My recommendation is *"How To Audition For the Musical Theater: A Step-By-Step Guide to Effective Preparation"* by Donald Oliver. This book saved my life when it came to musical theater auditions. It is simply amazing.

For theater, prepare your monologue based on your research of the show. If you are auditioning for the Cowardly Lion in The Wizard of Oz, you can rent the movie or watch clips on YouTube of the play. Then you can understand the play's specific comedy style, and have a better understanding of what song to choose. You might decide to go with a ballad because you discovered that the Cowardly Lion's solo is a ballad. You may decide to go with something comedic for your monologue because you learned that the show's style is comedic and expressive.

Researching monologues for film is similar to researching them for theater. The casting call will often have specifications for your monologue. It might ask for a "30-60 sec dramatic monologue" or "a 1 min monologue of your choice." Choose your monologue based on the audition's specifications and the tone of the project.

One time, I was auditioning for a girl who was kidnapped and escaping her abuser. Based on the storyline and information in the breakdown, I chose a short, 30 second monologue in which a girl talks to her abusive father. I chose the monologue because it suited the emotion and setting of the story. I knew it would show them that I was capable of that emotional range. By the time I finished the audition, they were very pleased with my audition and monologue choice.

If I had not paid attention to the storyline, I might have brought in a comedic monologue. Imagine: I brought in a monologue where a girl yells at her mom for taking her hair brush! It may have been an emotional and dramatic piece, but it would not have fit the general "vibe" or "tone" of the storyline. Doing my research helped me pick a monologue that suited the role.

Choose a monologue that is SHORTER than the allotted time, especially for a dramatic project. Actors often choose a monologue that is too long. When the actor times the monologue at home, it works, but when they perform it in the audition room, they go over the allotted time. Or, they rush the monologue through important pauses to finish in time. Pick a shorter monologue. It allows you to slow down, and take pauses in your monologue.

Also, some directors can be very strict in enforcing time restrictions. If you go over, they may cut you off right at one minute. Be sure to time yourself. Lastly, casting directors only need 10-20 seconds of your monologue to assess your acting talent. You do not need a long speech!

For film auditions, chose a contemporary monologue written for film and television. Contemporary monologues are monologues written in the past 20 years. For Shakespearean plays, choose a "classical" monologue. For other plays, chose a monologue that matches the play's genre/tone/time period.

However, avoid monologues that are famous and well-known. For example, if you do Hailee Steinfield's monologue from "The Edge of 17," or a Matt Damon's monologue from "Good Will Hunting," a lot of other actors will be bringing in the same monologue! Casting directors may subconsciously compare your performance to the original actor's.

Try to choose monologues that are active and are telling a story, "I remember when my mom used to..." are less active than ones that are happening in the present moment: "STOP taking my stuff mom!! I cannot take it anymore!" Both kinds of monologues can be useful, but active monologues are more powerful.

Twenty-One

How To Find a Monologue

I t may seem overwhelming to find a monologue, but they are a lot easier to find than you may think. So how can you find a monologue? Here are my genius, very sneaky tricks to find monologues.

My first tip for monologue discovery is to go on YouTube and search for "monologue competitions" or "monologue showcase" or "monologues for auditions" or "teen female monologues." Watch some monologues, and transcribe the monologues you want to perform.

Sneaky trick number two is one of my favorite tricks because it reminds me of where I came from. When I started acting, my family was too broke to afford books. Since I was short on money, I went to local libraries and bookstores. I looked through all the monologue books, and I took pictures of all the monologues I wanted to use in the future. Later, when I needed a monologue, I would flip through the pictures on my phone, and type up the ones I wanted to use. Suddenly, I had hundreds of free monologues.

So go to a library or bookstore and look through their acting books and plays. When you find something you like, take a picture. You can type it up later, or memorize it from your phone. This has worked so well for me, and I have HUNDREDS of photos of monologues on my phone. Just remember that monologues in monologue books are often longer than what is needed for a typical audition. But they are great to practice with or to alter for auditions.

People in the industry may not approve of my sneaky trick number three, but I am going to tell you guys anyway. After a few years in acting, I began to write my *own* monologues for auditions. Industry experts often tell actors that they should not write their own monologues. Casting directors can often tell when an actor has written their monologue, so this is not always the best route.

However, writing my own material has helped me a lot. I booked two roles in the past year with two monologues that I had written. And I love writing my own material. I can write a monologue that perfectly suits whatever audition I have. In my writing, I can be honest and share from a script that resonates with me. Writing makes you a better storyteller, and being a better storyteller makes you a better actor.

My sneaky tip number four is to research monologues online. In the bac of this book, I have listed some great monologue and commercial script websites, so be sure to check them out! And there are tons more to be found by googling "monologues for teens", and experimenting with different key words.

Lastly, my sneaky trick number five is to find monologues, scripts, and commercials from TV and movies. If you see a character that plays your type, and they are talking for a while without being uninterrupted, pause the Netflix and type their lines up. I have a note on my phone called "Monologues". I have written down a wide range of monologues from Euphoria, Grownish, and Disney shows.

I started finding monologues this way years ago. The first time I remember typing up a monologue was when I was fifteen, and I was watching this Disney movie *Zapped*. Right at the beginning, Zendaya does a fantastic monologue. I chose to type up her monologue because Zendaya's character was similar to characters I could audition for. Once I finished writing it down, I had a fun comedic monologue that I could use for practice, acting class, my acting profiles, or even an audition.

2019, filming a monologue I wrote about teen pregnancy in acting class

Twenty-Two

Working on Your Material

⚬❦⚬

*A*fter you have prepared the rest of your audition material, now, it is time to prepare for your performance. Here is where you get to really know your character, the story, and the lines. Here are my guidelines and tips for having the best performance in the audition room.

Use An Acting Coach

My first recommendation is to use an acting coach for auditions. An acting coach will watch and critique your performance and improve your audition technique. They will ask you questions designed to deepen your performance and take it to a more polished place.

I worked with an audition coach, Gloria Garayua, for my first ever feature film audition. The movie is called Camp Tough Love and it is available on Amazon Prime. She first watched me perform my monologue and then asked me some questions. Her questions were designed to help me think about who my character was.

Because the character was traumatized in the scene, she took me through the process of visualizing what the character was doing and seeing and feeling. "Imagine your character," she would say "and try to imagine all the stuff that they have been through." She also told me to picture who I was talking to, because it would make my acting more believable. She helped me become more comfortable with the script and develop my acting. I booked the audition, and I think that was because of her!

Do Your Background Prep

You must develop your character so you can perform well in your audition. However, this chapter is not to present you with a researched acting formula. There are many many ways to work on your material and there are many schools of acting techniques and trains of thought, so be sure to supplement your craft with acting classes. Acting is a study, and there is much more to it than what I will cover in this book. These skills take actors years to develop.

What I have laid out are the basic ABCs of script breakdown and character development. Here are some general guidelines to help you approach your script. Take what works for you.

When working on my background, the first thing I do is spend a lot of time reading the script to understand the story. So read any available script and background information. You have two objectives as you read the script: to understand the story, especially your scenes, and to understand the character. It is imperative to find every small bit of information and incorporate it into your performance. A careful read-through of the script will help you know not to give a dramatic teary-eyed performance when the script actually requires a more lighthearted performance.

Information about who the character is will be found in the description and dialogue. Observe what your character says about themselves and what other characters say about them, for clues about their personality.

Create a character bio. A character bio is a document where you write down facts about your character from the script. Use "I" statements as you write down who your character is and why. Using the "I" POV will help you identify with the role and get into your part.

Relationships

Investigating the RELATIONSHIP (s) is a big part of developing your character and dissecting the script. The "Relationships" are the character's connection to other characters in the scene. When looking at relationships, you need to find the answers to the questions below (and related) questions:

- How are the characters in the scene related to each other?
- How do they treat each other? How close are they? Are they mad at each other about anything? Do they love each other?
- How well they know the other person? What important memories, good or bad, do they have together?

When you are delivering your audition, it is also essential to visualize another person. Have you ever watched a monologue that seems fake and empty? Look at the actors' eyes. Their eyes are often wandering, glazed over, and the character appears to be aware that this is an act. You do not believe them as you watch them.

So you must have a clear picture of the person you are talking to, as a part of developing Relationships. In a self-tape, pick an actor you can envision playing that part. When you perform, imagine them standing across from you. Pick a spot where their eyes are, and imagine that you are saying your lines to them. This will make your auditions much more believable.

Backstory

When preparing for your scene, you also need to make choices about your characters' backstory. You can't go too in depth when creating a backstory for an audition, because you do may not know everything about the character and you do not want to play the character wrong. So make choices about their backstory that are supported by the information given to you.

Sometimes I will make backstory choices that are not found in the script, but only if I strongly feel that my choices make sense with the story. For example, I recently auditioned for a TV show on a huge streaming service. I knew that my character was alone and on the run. I researched online and I found out that the script was based on a book.

Through some research, I found out that in the book, my character's adopted family had abused her. I visualized the specifics of the abuse in my head, so I could have those vivid memories close to the surface of my performance. My backstory creation was more in-depth than I needed to go, but I knew that my acting choices were substantiated by the research I had done about the story.

After you book the part, then you create a full backstory. Start from the very beginning of the character's life — write down their childhood, their home life, their relationships with their parents, siblings, other family family, best friends, and impactful people in their life. If you want, choose a picture of an actor for each significant person in the character's life. Just as you know the face of your parents or your best friend, you should know the faces of the people in your character's life.

Write down and live through their core memories in their life. Know their personality and interests. When you book the part, spend a lot of time developing and really knowing who your character is as a 3D human being.

Objective

Next, many acting schools suggest that you should find the character's OBJECTIVE in the scene. An objective is the characters' goal in the scene. Objectives are typically articulated with transitive verbs, aka "to (verb)."

Let us say that you are doing a scene where, your character, has just found out that their girlfriend is cheating. In the scene, your character calls her. Instead of telling the girlfriend that he knows the truth, he may ask her passive aggressive questions to get her to confess of her own free will. His actions are fueled by an underlying objective "to get my girlfriend to confess."

Some teachers suggest that objectives like "get my girlfriend to confess"

154

are motivated by more "base" emotions. Base emotions are the more base desires that human beings have like love or security or power. For example, an attempt to get your girlfriend to confess could be more basely motivated by "getting my girlfriend **to love me** (enough to tell the truth)." When you look for the objective you ask:

- What is my character's goal?
- What are they trying to get from the other person?
- What are the stakes?
- Why do they want this goal?

While objectives can be a useful thing to think about , some other acting schools completely reject objectives. They argue:

"People do not enter into conversations or situations thinking about an objective. Why do actors need to prepare it?"

When actor care too much on about an objective, they could potentially derail their scene by making their objective too obvious. Instead, some schools and teachers suggest preparing with "I am" statements. For example, "I am hurt" and "I am in love" could be a good way of preparing for a scene where a guy is trying to get his girlfriend to confess. To me, both ways of looking at the script seem totally valid. I believe that an actor must study different ways to approach a scene, and figure out what sorts of tools work for them. So test it, try it, and play around with it.

Tactics

You can also look at the TACTICS. The tactics are *how* a character attempts to achieve their objective. Tactics are actions. In a scene where a boy is asking a girl to go out with him (objective), he may try different tactics to get what he wants. First, he might compliment her. Then he might point out how awful her boyfriend is. Then he might confess. All of these are different "tactics" that he uses to get his objective.

I did a scene with my acting coach, where a girl wants her father to rescue her from the cops, who are going to take her to her grandparents' house. She tries many "tactics" to convince her dad to save her. She begs, pleads, guilts him; she tries to reason with him; she tries everything she thinks will work. Those are "tactics". How the character tries to get what they want.

Again, some people disapprove of actors using tactics. In real life, people often do not consciously think of tactics to get what we want? Not often. Why should actors do that? But I like the idea of tactics as a way of breaking down the script and reading more into the character and how they think. Again, this is a tool for you to play around and use. Practice will help you refine your choices.

Environment

You need to be familiar with the characters' environment, in their scene and daily life. I like to think of a character's environment as the history of their relationship with their day to day life and their socioeconomic background:

Where do they go regularly, and why?

Who do they see regularly and why makes an impact in their life? (an abusive father, an influential teacher)

What is their daily schedule?

Are they rich or poor?

What is their worldview and why?

The environment is also looking at what the character's five senses are experiencing in the scene, and their historical relation to the place. Who the character is will influence how they interact with the environment.

For example, in Game of Thrones (no spoilers, I promise. Although if you have not seen the show by now, shame!), a rich queen who gets thrown into a dungeon. She acts differently in the jail than the characters that she herself threw into the dungeon. Those other characters were used to hardships, but she was spoiled. So she acted really distraught and out of place.

A good actor will change their performance and how their character interacts with their environment based on the character's upbringing and historical environment. Here are some more questions to think about:

- Are they in their bedroom? In their parents' room? Jail?
- Is it cold or hot? Is it morning, night, or day? Weekend or weekday?
- How comfortable are they with that area?
- What is their relationship with their current setting?
- How long have they lived in that house, and how long have they been in that bedroom? What is important to them in the bedroom?
- Does that room/space make them feel more relaxed, tense, or something else?

Journalism Questions

Looking at the RELATIONSHIPS, OBJECTIVES, TACTICS, and ENVIRONMENT, is an excellent way to break down and understand a scene or character. Another way to approach these materials is to look at the "WHO WHAT WHERE WHY WHEN HOW?" of the scene.

- **WHO:** Who is in the scene? Who are they? (Personalities, background etc).
- **WHAT:** What is happening in the scene? What are the primary series of events of the story? What is the relationship of the characters to the other? What do they want from each other? What is in their way? What circumstances are the characters going through at the moment (injuries, alternative mental states, etc.)?
- **WHERE:** Where are they? What is their environment? What does it look like? What is around them? What information are they getting from their five senses?
- **WHY:** Why? Why do they want what they want? Why are they fighting

each other? Why are they in this situation? What is happening to the characters emotionally (it is often more than one thing. Someone can be angry, but also hurt and sad) the context? What is the history/series of events that happened leading up to this scene? You should live through the character's history before the scene. What happened right before this scene started?

- **WHEN:** When? What period is this set in? What is their social status? How has their upbringing/quality of life influenced who they are? What is the date? What is the time of the day? Does this affect them in the scene?
- **HOW:** How? How are they fighting for what they want? What tactics do they use? How do they fight for each other?

If you are doing a monologue from a movie/play, you can read the script or watch the movie up until the script or monologue appears. That will help you answer the questions above. While preparing for an audition, think about these questions and make conscious choices. Once you have done these preparation steps, you are ready for memorization!

Twenty-Three

How to Memorize Your Lines

*H*ere are my memorization guidelines to help you get that script word perfect! Although, I think it is essential to know that there are no quick and easy steps to memorizing anything. Memorization means dedicating time and focusing on committing the words to your brain. It is a skill, and you have to practice. The more you memorize, the easier it gets.

The earlier you start memorizing and the more time you spend, the more memorized you will be. After you read this chapter, I also encourage you to look at the memorization techniques online. There are many available resources, and you should experiment with different ones.

How to Memorize Your Lines

- Be positive! Tell yourself that you are capable You can learn more than you think is possible. Memorization is a skill that you can improve! But you have to give your brain a chance.
- "LineLearner" is an app that you can download and it is great for memorizing scripts. It costs about three or four dollars. Many of my actor friends have recommended it to me and told me that it was essential to their preparation process. I now use it, because I can record my lines and play them back. This flexibility lets me memorize my lines in the car, or while I'm cleaning my room.
- Write your lines out by hand! It is scientifically proven that we learn better when we write things down, by hand, on paper. You use a different part of the brain for handwriting and speaking aloud, than reading on a screen. Actually, for the first year of my acting class, I wrote out all of my scripts. My acting teachers *hated* when I brought in scripts handwritten, but it helped me memorize them. Eventually, memorizing became easier and I did not have to write them out anymore, but it took me years.
- Try moving around while you memorize your lines! The movement will help jog your memory.
- Connect the words to something visual. If your character is recounting a memory or telling a story, spend some time imagining that memory, so your brain thinks that it really happened. Going through the memories will make your lines easier to remember, because as you perform you can recount the "memory". If your character is reciting a list, imagine every item on that list. Try and find out whether or not your character has an emotional or memorable connection to the items on the list. You will find that the lines come to you so much easier!

- RehearsalPro is another app I have heard is useful. I have never tried it, and it is more expensive than LineLearner, at $20.00, but it could have some valuable features.
- Have someone check your lines. Checking your lines mean giving someone else the script and say your lines to them. Sometimes when we practice by ourselves, we cheat, and look at the lines. And now we've tricked ourselves into thinking we remember more than we actually do. Practicing with others will show you how memorized you truly have the lines.

Memorizing a Monologue

Monologues can be harder to memorize because monologues are just giant blocks of text. So for this section, I thought it would be helpful to demonstrate how *I* learn my monologues because I sometimes use a particular process that helps me.

First, I do the acting background work. I know what is going on in the scene. I have visuals, memories, history, and faces to help me know who I am talking to, and what I am talking about in the monologue. Preparing my backstory makes memorization so much easier.

When I've finished the backstory, I read the monologue aloud several times so to get a good sense of the order of the words. However, I do read the speech in a monotone way because I do not want to rehearse any tone or inflections. I only wish to repeat the words aloud.

If the monologue is really long, I will create an outline of the general progression of thoughts. Each bullet point is a transition to a new thought. I will number the different thought and memorize the outline briefly. For example, let's say I am learning a monologue from episode 1 season 1 of Euphoria. Rue is talking to Fez at a party, asking him to be her drug dealer. My outline for that monologue looks like this:

1. "I am 11 years old, my dad's diagnosis good"
2. "To celebrate we ordered Chinese food"

3. "Sitting with my parents and suddenly can't breathe"
4. "Gasping → call ambulance →I thought allergic reaction"
5. "Valium to calm me down → this is it"
6. "Two year later he was gone panic stayed – I found a way to live"

When I finish outlining, I memorize one section at a time. I start with the first section, and I repeat all the lines in the first section over and over. I move on when I can recite that first section three times in a row perfectly. Once my first section is memorized, I go to the second section.

If there is a particular part of any section that I keep messing up on, I repeat that part several times. I also try to either visualize the scenario, make a cute little rhyme, or do something unique to help me remember the progression of words. For example, if a line is full of adjectives like, "He was a big, hungry, mean, bald man," I repeat to myself "BHMB" and visualize those letters. I associate BHMB with that part. When I get to that line, I remember "BHMB", the order of the words I am supposed to recite.

When I have memorized the first and second section, I try to recite them both together. Then I learn the third section, and then the fourth section. I then say section #3 and #4 together as a pair. Then I recite section 1-4 all together. I keep going until I finish the monologue. When I finish, I try to recite the whole thing, looking down at my outline if I forget.

Once I have worked through the whole monologue using these methods, I would probably pause for the day. The next day, I try to say the entire thing 3-5 times without looking at the paper.

More General Guidelines for Memorization

Along with memorizing the lines, your mouth needs to memorize the lines as well. Although you should not rehearse how you are going to say the line, your mouth should have it memorized so the mouth knows where to go and the words come easy.

Scripts with another partner can be easier to memorize because you have the other person's lines to cue your lines. But you can use this memorization system for scripts as well as monologues. Instead of using sections, you can split your script by pages.

When you perform, always listen to what the other character is saying before saying your lines. reacting. Too often, actors react, say their lines, and then worry about their next line while the other person is talking. Then they are distracted from the scene, and are dead water, not acting in between lines. Listen and pay close attention to the other character when they speak. This will help you organically remember your lines. Follow your character's thought process from the other character's line to your next line.

The last crucial step when memorizing your lines is performing your material. Recite the whole thing in front of your family or your camera. Reciting it in front of others is the best way you could practice. Recitation most accurately simulates an audition. It can be scary to perform in front of people who know you, but it is scary to perform in front of casting directors. So having others watch you is like a dress rehearsal.

If you do not have any family members or friends available, film yourself. Set up your phone, webcam or camera, and perform in front of that. Filming yourself is an excellent way to get a realistic preview of your performance.

The most important thing when it comes to memorization is:

Do Not Rehearse.

Do not rehearse your emotions or facial expressions in the mirror or a certain line. Rehearsing in the mirror makes you focus on your looks, not your actual acting. And when you practice inflections and emotions, you lock yourself into a performance. Your performance becomes stale and not spontaneous. So when I memorize, I say my lines monotone and flat, like a robot. I add the inflections and notes only when perform.

You may have instincts of what to do with certain lines, and you can take note of your gut. But in real life, you do not practice your responses. Your reactions just come naturally from your internal conflicts. Your performance, as well, should come our naturally.

164

FAQ: *Do I have to have my script memorized when I go to an audition?*

A good rule of thumb is: the the more memorized you are, the better. If you receive a script more than 24 hours before the audition, you are expected to be memorized. If you get the audition less than 24 hours before, try to be as memorized as possible. But in such short notice, it is more important to be familiar with your script and your character.

If you are doing a monologue, you should be completely off-book (memorized) When you perform a monologue, you are also not going to hand the casting director a script for them to keep track of your lines. They are trusting that you are 100% memorized.

If you can only have some of the script memorized, always memorize

- The first line
- The last line
- Any important speeches

You want to have the first and last lines memorized because these are moments where you should be looking up and connecting with the reader so the casting director can see your face. Also, there is often a section in any audition scene where your character has an important line or speech. Try and have this memorized as well. This is an impactful moment, and so you want to do it off the page. Those are key moments to commit to memory.

No matter how memorized you are, do not worry about making mistakes. You do not have to say every word correctly. If you mess up a word or pronunciation in the audition, it is fine. Just correct yourself, as you would in real life, and move on. Do not underline your mistakes by making any faces or frustrated noises. The casting director may not have even noticed your errors. If you switch or forget a line, and you are on the first page of the script, you can ask to start over. But if you are past the first page, keep going. Be sure to look up any words you do not know how to say.

During your audition with a scene partner, keep your script in your hand, even if you are completely memorized. In auditions, actors often blank and forget the lines. You do not want to pause the audition by going to get your script and then coming back. Keeping your script in your hand makes casting directors feel at ease, because they do not have to worry about you blanking and not knowing the line.

During the audition, turn the pages along with the scene. If you suddenly blank, find your line on the page and keep going. Keep your script at chest level, and hold it in the hand closest to your scene partner. If you are reading with the casting director, and there is a camera, hold the script in the hand furthest from the camera.

Your biggest priority is to have your audition go relatively smoothly. Memorization and bringing in your script will help you accomplish that.

Twenty-Four

Vocal Tips For Actors

*A*s actors, our body is our instrument. We need to have a well-tuned tool. This means taking care of our face, voice, and body so we can use them to perform better. Be sure to pay attention to how you are using your voice throughout your career. Seek professional help if needed. Experts recommend that all actors have a daily vocal practice for maintenance and improvement. Here are my tips, and I also suggest you looking into professional help.

When you practice your lines, work on your pronunciation. I have always struggled with pronunciation. I speak faaaaast and I mumble certain words. When I was younger, I also had my parents' Nigerian accent. You may still hear hints of it to this day. I must constantly force myself to slow down, exaggerate my speech, and make my lips move more.

If you get "slow down" as a common critique in real life or in an acting class, practice! It is a habit you can overcome. My best enunciation tip came from my mom: my mom would remind me - "when you feel like you are exaggerating too much, that is when you have just started to slow down enough. Really slow your enunciation down.

In my first movie, Abitha, my line goes by so fast because I speed talked through the whole thing. I did not think I was talking quickly at the time, but I was. *And that was my only line in the movie.* So much for my time to shine. Ensure that this does not happen to you. Take your time! Enjoy your pauses. Take deep breaths. Enunciate! Record and listen to yourself talking and practice daily.

If you have a problem with stuttering and saying certain words, practice saying the words with a pencil in your mouth. This will make you over enunciate when you practice the lines, and when you take the pencil out, pronouncing the words become easier.

Look up how to say confusing or unknown words before you go into an audition. There is no point in pronouncing a word wrong, or with the wrong inflection because you did not know how to say it, or what it means. We have so many resources. Google it!

Breathe during your lines. There are almost always pauses and moments in your script. Before you start your scene, take a deep breath. Throughout the scene, find use these moments to take deep breaths into your diaphragm.

Always warm-up before performing. I love using Amy Walker's Vocal warm-ups. I have talked about her a few times in this book and it is BECAUSE I think she is truly an invaluable resource. Amy Walker's YouTube Channel helped my speech, diction, and vocal resonance. She warms up your body, face, and mouth and tongue to maximize the clarity of your performance. She also has fantastic American Accent Tutorials that I really recommend.

Many people reading this book come from all over the world. And even in America we all have our regionalities, and slight (or not so slight) accents. However, in 99% of Hollywood movies, the actors have "plain accents". Casting directors are looking for people with standard Californian accents. Amy Walker's tutorials can help you perfect your English accent.

If you have a strong accent, I suggest regularly working on your English accent, doing tongue twisters, or working with a dialect coach. Even if you do not need this work, as actors, we should all be warming up our body and face daily, and working on proper breathing, posture, and stance techniques. Start looking into what works for you.

TIP: If you have an accent, and you can switch back and forth between that accent and your English accent, put that on your resume! Continue to work at getting better at both of those accents. I have more diction exercises and Amy Walker's Youtube Channel in the Appendix.

recording a Youtube Video at an Actual Studio

Twenty-Five

Timeline of Audition Prep

*Y*ou have a week until your audition. What should you start doing? This chapter is a step by step timeline of each day leading up to your audition.

The Week Before the Audition

A week before your audition is when you should start the time eating more fruits and veggies, and consuming less dairy and sugar. Regulating your diet helps decrease pimples! Healthy eating also helps avoid getting acne ON your audition day.

A healthy diet has benefits apart from vanity. Nutritious eating will help you stay focused, work on your script and have energy for your performance. You will feel better overall!

Start working on your monologue, script, or song at LEAST a week before your audition. Do your background work, research, and begin memorizing.

Start planning your outfit, and see if you will need to buy new clothes. Go shopping for any audition outfit or accessories that you may need.

Two Days Before your Audition

Start drinking lots of water! Perform your monologue in front of friends and family. Evaluate your performance and see if there is anything that you need to tweak. Print out your headshots and resume. Make a list of anything you might need to bring.

The Night Before

I like to go to sleep with a light coconut oil mask, so my skin is soft and glowing in the morning. But again, do not try anything new on your skin. You do not want to irritate your skin. And get LOTS of sleep. You do not want eye bags and you do want as much energy as possible. Although auditions are short, they really drain you.

Drink water, but not too much. You do not want to be running to the bathroom every five seconds. Eat a semi-light dinner for a nice sleep. Avoid consuming anything diary-based. Dairy coats your throat and creates mucusy speech. Do not eat anything you have not tried before.

Prepare. Lay your clothes out. Pack the stuff you need to take with you in the car, using my handy checklist in Chapter 19. Print out directions. Charge your phone. If you want, stretch before you sleep! This will help you rest. Practice your lines before going to bed. When you practice your lines right before you go to sleep, you remember them better.

On the Day of the Audition

STRETCH. Everything: your face, neck, torso, your hands, knees, feet. You can find a full-body stretch video on YouTube. When I was younger, I liked doing a few jumping jacks and pushups before I headed off to the car to get my blood flowing. But you do not have to be as fanatical as me. A light warm-up is sufficient. And please, do not overexert yourself!

WARM UP THE VOCALS. I used to do two vocal warm-ups: a facial warm-up with some tongue twisters and then, a pre-choir warm-up.Make silly faces. Hum. Do not be afraid to wake some stiff old muscles up!

EAT A HEALTHY, ENERGY PROVIDING BREAKFAST. Eat something

"whole" and "hearty" and easy on the stomach to get long-lasting energy. Go for the fruit, oatmeal, eggs, avocado toast, and the nuts. Be sure to avoid dairy, including milk and chocolate. Drink LOTS of water.

CHECK YOUR STUFF! Double-check your list and make sure you have everything. Remember your headshot, resume, and directions.

LEAVE EARLY! I have learned that when it comes to auditions, you can leave early, and STILL end up late. It can be *impossible* to find the building or you might run into an accident. So play it safe. Leave to arrive 45 mins early. Auditions where I leave 45 mins early, I always end up arriving precisely on time. I also do not feel last-minute stress, because I gave myself enough time to find where I am supposed to be. Getting there early helps, especially if you are in an area that you do not recognize.

However, do not come to an audition or set too early. If you are there thirty minutes earlier or more, wait in like a local coffee shop or something till about 15 minutes beforehand.

REVIEW YOUR SCRIPT. Review it like three times. Once you are in the car, leave it alone. You are good

BRING A GOOD ATTITUDE!!

having fun during my acting class

Twenty-Six

How to Deal with Audition Nerves

I am very passionate about the intersections between mental health and acting, because I believe that a healthy inner life is essential for longevity and purpose in this career. The best way to prepare for any audition is to bring a positive mental attitude.

I made a video called "How to Deal With Audition nerves," and I have transcribed that video for you guys here. I want you to read this chapter before every audition or even every day! It is meant to calm any doubts about your audition. Best of Luck!

Having a Good Attitude for Auditions

Hey, you guys! It is Marie here. I hope you are having a beautiful day. If you are the kind of person who gets really nervous before auditions, performances, or any instance where you get up in front of people, this is the chapter for you.

Every performer, at least the human ones, can relate to that crippling fear of auditioning and performing. We are scared of messing up, being judged, failing. We want our dream so bad: the role, the agent, the applause. And our desire to do well can make us extremely anxious.

I have been through every kind of nervousness, and I am here to tell you how to overcome your audition nerves so that you can be the most kick...donkey for your performance.

To conquer your nerves, you first have to accept them. Realistically you will probably always get nervous. We may have insecurities that will haunt us for the rest of our lives. The trick is to not let them control you. Nerves are a good thing, because they are a sign that you care. So don't shame yourself or feel out of place because you get nervous. Your nerves, your past, your thoughts, have no power to make you freeze up and perform anything less than your most confident self. You have control over your thoughts, and your brain does what you tell it to do. It is ok to be nervous. Your nerves just cannot beat you.

Did you know that feeling nervous and feeling excited is the same physiologically? Your body can not tell the difference between the feelings. The only difference is the story you tell your brain. So if you tell your mind that you are only excited, you will change your perspective. Your body will believe it, and you will begin to feel excited.

Regulate your breathing. When I am very nervous, I pause, and I breathe. I breathe, I gather mental images and words of my nerves, fears, insecurities. When I breathe out, I imagine myself releasing it all. Another good breathing exercises is to trace the rectangular outline of your phone with your finger while breathing. As you trace the length, breathe in. Over the width, hold, and then on the other long side breathe out. Keep doing that to calm your nerves.

Mentally, you need to release your fear. Let all your doubts and negative thoughts go gently from your focus. Realize that you cannot control what happens in the audition room. You can not control whether the casting director likes you, or if you get the part. So to have a successful audition, you just have to focus on yourself and your performance. Do not worry about trying to impress anyone.

If you need, repeat this mantra:

"I cannot control what happens in the audition room. The only thing that I can control is my attitude, my confidence, and the fact that I strive to do my best."

Begin to use your imagination. Imagine going into the audition room and doing a good job. Imagine how happy you will be once you have had an excellent performance. Picture how excited you will be once you get the part. Using your imagination on fortunate circumstances will help attract them into your life.

Preparation helps get rid of anxiety. Know who you are performing for. Sometimes I "stalk" the casting company on social media, and then I recognize all their faces in person. It kind of gives me power, because I know them before they even know me! Another way to prepare is to have a mock audition or dress rehearsal. It really helps get rid of nerves.

Before the audition, do things that make you feel positive! Walk outside. Point out the things that make you happy outside. Listen to music. Make a list of the positive things about your audition. Do things that make you laugh.

I love to talk to myself before an audition. I affirm that I am a wonderful, confident, and unique person. I have to make myself believe good things about myself, otherwise I would be too nervous to perform. I list all the things that I am scared about, and I myself imagine letting them go. I breathe deeply several times and talk myself logically through my self-doubt. I watch YouTubers that make me happy, like Lilly Singh or Tana Mongeau. I watch motivational videos. I dance. Anything to relax, breathe, talk to myself, and put myself in the right mood.

Lastly, be grateful! This audition is exciting! You audition represents a new experience for you, so get hyped!! No matter what happens, it is going to be amazing. Go for the learning! Go for the journey.

I really want everyone who reads this book to know how unique and beautiful and wonderful they are. No one else in that audition room is better than you. No one is more special, more talented, more beautiful, more charming, or luckier than you. Even the casting director is a human, just like you. You have something amazing to offer. Take a deep breath and trust that. Believe that you can do it.

Know that auditions are just auditions. There will another better audition coming up at any moment. Of course, auditioning will be scary and very nerve-wracking. It is hard to put yourself out there. But you can do it. I am very proud of you for getting this audition and facing this challenge. Genuinely, I wish you the best of luck. Much love.

Twenty-Seven

The Best Advice for Auditions

y best audition advice comes from my own audition stories. As you might guess, not all of my auditions have been successful. In fact, some of them have ended up pretty badly. However, I learned a lot from every one of them. I think you guys will too.

The Time I Dorked Out

The first bad audition that I will tell you about in this chapter happened when I was with my first agency. My first agency was a scammy agency. They have a legitimate business, but they scammed their actors into buying useless classes, and going to fake auditions. In Chapter 33, I will talk more about how to avoid getting scammed.

My agency did one thing well. Every month or so, they would fly in an agent or casting director or manager from LA to give us "talent auditions." I am not sure how much opportunity was available in these auditions, but the people being flown in were credible. These were casting directors and agents who had cast and represented actors from on Disney, Nickelodeon, and more. So, the auditions were a big deal, even though the visitors were paid to attend.

One day, I learned that my agency was flying in this agent who was going to evaluate our auditions, give us advice, and perhaps 'scout' a few of us. My agency told me that if that agent represented us, she would submit us for auditions in LA while we still lived in the Midwest. I googled her, and she had some impressive clients. I was ecstatic.

When I first arrived there were, like, forty kids and teens in the common room. I recall looking around super enviously. There were *so many girls* my age, and they all looked like Victoria Secret Models. They had perfect face proportions and straight silky hair. My heart beat faster when I saw them because these Amazonian goddesses were the perfumed models I have never been.

The audition instructions were simple: Go into the room and read the script they gave you outside. I had also done a few auditions with this agency before, so I was not a complete newbie. But for some reason, that day, everything was just piling up. The number of 'competitors', the stakes. I was super freaked out.

As I was in the main room, practicing, my mom tried to encourage me to loosen up. She asked if I was going to add any hand gestures or movements, so my acting wasn't too stiff. I blew her off. I was too focused on everyone else, and I could not take in her suggestions. For example, there was a little boy ahead of me. I kept watching him practice. *He's so charismatic and young,* I thought. *He is reading that script like he is an experienced Nickelodeon Disney commercial TV actor.*

Finally, we all lined up, and there were like thirty kids in front of me, creating a line of parents and kids that wrapped around the large room. I could not look to my left or my right without seeing a kid practicing his lines, or a parent coaching the kids on their inflections. I was intimidated by the competition surrounded me. The audition door room was also open, so as I got further up in line, I could see who went before me, how they performed, and hear the agent's feedback. The audition felt like a checkout line. A person went up, got critiqued, and meandered out the back door. We were being treated like cattle, and I hated it. As I absorbed the whole room, I gulped inwardly and went back to practicing my script.

My mom and I waited in line, headshot, and resume in hand. Finally, I walked in and handed the assistant my headshot and resume. By the time I got to the audition room, I was feeling so inferior that I doubted the stuff I already knew. And my doubts were becoming obvious. For example, I asked the agent, "Where do I stand again?". Silence. I looked over. There was a giant white obvious X on the floor, and lights surrounding a spot where I clearly should have been standing. Oopsie. But that was just the beginning.

Before I started reciting the lines, I again... paused. I asked the agent, "Do you want me to slate?" I had already known that I was supposed to slate. But I was trying to tip toe through the audition, and do everything perfect. She told me to slate, in a tone that I interpreted to be mild annoyance, and so I did. Then I performed.

I had hoped that at least my performance would be redeeming, even if the rest of my audition wasn't. I mean, I had acted in two short films before this point. I thought that I was pretty good and that I could float through on my natural talent like I always did. But her feedback was biting. I do not remember exactly what she said, but here were her main points:

1. I needed more training
2. I was way too stiff.
3. Overall my audition was...underwhelming

I walked out of that audition feeling defeated. I was second-guessing my place in this business. I had auditioned for a certified, accredited "LA person", and I walked out knowing she would never remember me because my performance was mediocre at best. I felt so down about how I had ruined my opportunity.

But my mom was pretty upbeat, as she always is. She told me that I just needed to loosen up and work on my acting. She made the solution seem simple. "You will work on it and get better," she told me. "Now you know what happens. Next time you will be more prepared." And she was right.

I learned from that audition, and I prepared. I was never as stiff in another audition. I tried to never ask pointless questions and I always faked confidence in following auditions. In my very next audition for that agency, I was a lot more prepared. I got accepted to a showcase, and they wanted to take me to LA. I learned from that experience and I became so much more comfortable being myself. And I never let myself be as intimidated by competition as I was on that day.

the duo of my mom and I, walking back to the car after a photoshoot

Lessons To Learn

You will have bad auditions. It is inevitable. Auditions can be great or bad or mediocre. Never to let a lousy audition get to you and make you doubt your talent. Listen to the words of my mom. One day does not equal a bad life, and one bad audition does not equal a bad actor or failed career. Choose to learn from your mistakes. Let them fuel you and spur you to improve. Do not give up. If I had given up on acting then when I wanted to give up, I would not be where I am now.

Do not let yourself get intimidated by the competition. My mom drilled this into me:

"Your competition is *just like you*. Maybe worse."

My martial arts instructor would always say:

"No one is better than you and you are better than no one".

There may be a gorgeous person who has done beauty pageants since they were four, but you know what? Beauty is overrated. You are still unique and amazing. You have something valuable to offer the casting director, even though it may not feel like it. Act with confidence.

RELAX! RELAX! I used to tighten up in my auditions. I would get stuck in my head and try to psych myself up for a perfect performance. However, this would hurt my chances. People do not want to see you try to act. They do not want to see you work yourself into an actor frenzy and attempt to get every word perfect. They want to know that it is easy for you to get into character.

When I started relaxing and doing auditions as if I was talking to my friend, I started booking jobs again. So now I force myself to relax. Do not take yourself seriously. Laugh at yourself. Be you. Get dirty, and make mistakes! Do not try to be perfect, because if you do, you will not show your true authentic self.

That Awkward Moment

One day, I came across this audition for a student-directed music video. I sent the producer this message:

Hello! My name is Marie Tagbo. I live here in **********! I play ages 14-17 I have been in a few short films, a commercial and music video, plus tons of theater performances! I would love to be able to work with you on this project :)
  My Youtube Channel:

https://www.youtube.com/channel/UCkVCuRAqk_KyLcniOVroFJQ

Headshots: link here

Thank you so much! I hope you had a great weekend, Marie

She emailed back, and introduced herself and the project. Then she gave me the audition time. And we only emailed about the audition times.

I arrived at the building, the student unlocked the door, and I went up into the elevator with her. In the elevator, she told me about herself and the project. She had this gorgeous afro, and I complimented her on her hair. She also complimented me on my hair. We chatted amiably until the elevator stopped.

We went inside this room. She had a camera set up, and some scripts on the table. She told me to stand in front of the camera and slate. Really straightforward. So I did. I was not entirely sure what to expect after I slated, but I assumed that she was going to give me a script to read. In her email, she gave no instruction about memorizing anything. So I had not prepared anything.

I slated, smiled, and then I waited. She looked at me, expectantly. I looked back at her, smiling. She said, "You can go ahead." Uh oh. Go ahead with what?

I told her I had nothing prepared. That was when she realized that she had forgotten to ask me to prepare a monologue. "So you don't have anything prepared, do?" she asked. "Nope." I replied. Why would I? She had no instructions about bringing in a monologue! And did she really not have *anything* else prepared for me to do?

The whole situation was so unfortunate because up until that point, the audition had been going well. She apologized profusely, and I apologized as well, but sadly, that was the end of the audition! She did not have anything more for me to do, and I had nothing to show her. She told me she could use my slate and decide the roles from there.

Lessons To Learn

Always be prepared. It was not my fault that she had forgotten to tell me to bring in a monologue. However, *I* am the one looking for a job. I could have prepared a monologue anyway, or emailed a follow-up question. Casting directors are looking for reasons to eliminate someone. And because she had not seen me act, I was easier to eliminate from her list.I learned that when things go wrong in an audition, I need to focus on what I can do to prevent it from happening again.

If I had come prepared, I could have impressed her. It would have been so cool if I had said, "Don't worry. You forgot? No problem, I always have two monologues memorized just in case." Preparation and confidence would have been so impressive, and her mistake would have been an opportunity for me to stand out.

Always have a couple of monologues performance-ready at any time. If a director tells you to prepare one monologue, prepare two. You do not need to inform them of the second monologue you prepared. But if they ask you if you have another monologue prepared, when you finish the first, it is your time to shine.

Another lesson I learned is to be careful about monologue choices. You may not want to send condescending, harsh, or shameful monologues to the casting director, especially about topics that you have touched on.

After the audition, my mom and I decided that it would be a good idea to send her another monologue. And that was is a good idea!

But I speculate that my monologue choice was faulty. I chose a monologue

I had been memorizing called "Hair." It was a socially charged monologue that criticized people who commented on black people's hair. And her and I had talked about hair in the elevator.

She could have interpreted this monologue as a jab toward the comments she had made about my hair earlier that day. After I sent that monologue, and she thanked me, and I never heard anything from her again. I have no idea what she thought about it. But you have to be very specific and strategic about your monologue choices.

The last thing I learned from this audition is never to assume why you did not get cast. Despite these unfortunate events, I do not know why I did not get cast. It could have been because I wasn't prepared, or I sent in a bad monologue, but you never know. You cannot assume.

Rejection is almost always never personal. I have had bad auditions where I got the part, and auditions with good feedback, where I got rejected. Sometimes you might not get the part because you are too tall. Maybe you are blonde, and they already have a blonde in the movie, and it would be confusing. So do not stress about it. Be happy to audition, and when you finish, leave the audition in the audition room.

My Audition Story About Someone Else

This story is not about me, which is lovely, because I was getting tired of sharing my failures. This story is about another girl who I observed while waiting in an audition room.

My current agent sent me on an audition for a paid commercial. I arrived, sat down, and met the casting director. After I introduced myself, he told me to wait, and he would call me up shortly. So I waited.

The audition room was in a reconstructed warehouse building, and the audition room was not enclosed or separated from the waiting room. Instead, the rooms were adjacent and sectioned off by a thin wall. Anyone in the waiting room could hear everything from the other side of the wall.

When I got to the audition room, the casting director did not give me a script to read while I waited, although the commercial was a cold read.

So while I was waiting in the audition room, all I could do was listen to the audition currently happened. I listened because I wanted to figure out what the script was about. So I started listening to the other girl perform. I'm going to be honest, her reading sounded so good. I could feel myself starting to get insecure, and so I had to continue encouraging myself.

After she finished, the director said something like "Not bad. Next time, read the lines so that you are not looking down at the page the whole time. Your paper is covering most of your face, and I cannot see your facial expressions." He was nice, but the way he delivered his feedback would make anyone feel nervous. She was my competition and even I felt worried for her.

She nervously accepted his criticism and he had her go again. She started reading it, and he stopped her. Again he reminded her to say the lines to the camera, not the paper. Halfway through the second read, it was apparent that she was not doing what he asked. He seemed super frustrated. She left the room in a hurry, with her head down as if she was about to cry.

Alright, Marie, I thought, *whatever you do, look **up** when you say your lines. Do NOT look down at the paper while reading your lines!!!!*

The casting director came out, had me sit down on another couch, and he gave me the lines to go over. He was super nice and even offered me some water. But I was terrified.

As I went over my lines, I knew I had to move fast and figure out my strategy. I did not try to memorize the script, knowing that trying to memorize for this cold read would be useless. I focused only on understanding the general idea of the scene. I was also feeling out how I would say certain parts. Five minutes later, he came and brought me into the audition room. I stood on the mark, slated, and took a deep breath. I started reading my lines. I let my lines come out choppy. Like this:

"Once upon a time there was -"

Look down at my paper, to get my next phrase. I did not start talking until I looked up at the camera.

"- a pretty princess who -"

Look down at page again. I did not start talking till I had the next phrase.

And for most of the audition, I spoke in fragments and pieces. I never talked while reading the script, and only started when I was facing the camera. I took pauses when I needed to. When I looked down, I tried to get a whole phrase or sentence, so my breaks were more natural. But the reading still felt super weird. But I knew I had to correctly do what the casting director had instructed the other girl to do.

After my first read-through, he gave me direction on how to read a specific line, and I reread the script. I was trying my best to apply what he asked. Afterward, he asked me about my availability, and I was done!

Lessons To Learn

The method that I used to read my script is called the "Cold Read Audition" technique. We will cover this technique in Chapter 28, but here is some valuable information:

Even though you are not memorized for a cold read audition, casting directors do not want to watch you perform to your paper. So pause when you are looking at the page reading your lines. Resist the urge to speak until you are looking back up at the camera or the reader. That way, when you perform the casting director can observe all of your expressions and emotions. Tips such as this are called "Audition Technique", or "Cold Read Audition Technique". You will learn and practice these techniques best in a class.

Learn from others. If I had auditioned and done the same thing that the other actress had done, the director probably would have been frustrated. My talent and skills were maybe even emphasized by her mistakes. Either way, I helped myself by paying attention and adjusting my performance based on what I had learned.

Listen to direction! If you are unable to listen to instruction, then the director will not want to cast you, even if you are talented. You need to be malleable, or else the director will be stuck with a performance he does not want. A casting director would rather hire someone less talented, who can be directed than someone who cannot take direction. It is better to be imperfect, than good but unchangeable.

I do not tell this story to shame or shade the actress because she was talented and gorgeous! But those things are not always enough. You need to have audition skill, and not just acting skill to get the part. Learn from my stories, other people's stories, from class, and other avenues so that you can improve your audition craft!

Twenty-Eight

How To Do a Cold Read

The following tips are helpful for any audition, but you should be especially aware of them during a cold read audition. In a cold read, your nerves may be running wild, and you may not know what to focus on or prioritize. Here is what you should do in a cold read:

Know The Basics. In a cold read, you might not have all the background information, so use whatever information you can find in the scene. Read the script three to four times to orient yourself in the story. Then, make choices on how you will approach the character. Go with your gut! Know the answers to important questions like:

Who is my character? What happens to them in this scene? Where are they? Why are they here and what do they want? How do they get it?

Be Comfortable With Silences. Find where there are moments and pauses in the script. Be comfortable with these pauses. There are silences in real life, and there are silences in film. These quiet moments can be really impactful, and new actors bulldoze through them instead of letting the moments happen. You have time. It is ok to let your character think, remember, and let emotions bubble up before responding.

Find the Moments to Face the Camera. There may be special moments in the script where the character is looking around or thinking. Find those moments, where your character is not talking directly to the other character and perform those moments more towards the camera.

Be Committed! In a cold read, you might not know the genre or the content of the material until you are in the waiting room. The script might be serious and dramatic, or light-hearted and comedic. It might ask you go to unexpected emotional places. The most important thing is to commit 100% to whatever you are asked to do. That confidence will help you book the role.

Have Your First Line Memorized. Commit your first and last line to memory. With these lines memorized, you can emotionally connect with your reader and have more of an impact when you say those lines. Memorization helps you start and end your audition strong.

Be Yourself! The best part about cold reads is that you have the freedom to follow your instincts and make mistakes. Trust yourself. Your gut is often more right than wrong! Bring yourself to the character. Perform the role the way *you* think that part should be performed.

Do Not Stay Glued To the Paper! I see so many new actors in my acting class make this mistake, so I am going to repeat this point. Actors need to let CDs see their eyes. You have more time than you think. Listen to the other character, then go down and read your lines, then say them. Do not blend these steps at all.

Practice Cold Reads. Now that you know the basics of cold read technique, you can practice and improve your skills! Download a scene from the Internet, or read from cereal boxes, books, and your phone. Pretend you are doing a cold read. Practice the motions of reading your lines, looking up and saying your line, and then looking back down and getting the next few lines.

Twenty-Nine

Tips for Acing Any Audition

going to my movie premiere

ere are my top tips for having a captivating audition that **wins the casting director over**, no matter your level of experience.

Enter the room with confidence! Confidence is what sets you apart. I like comparing acting to being a salesman. You are a salesman, but instead, you are the product. If you are not confident in you, how can others "buy" you? (By "buy" I mean like, hire you on set, not like, slavery. You get it, ok.)

196

Fake it till you make it. Own your imperfections. Know you are the best actor and actress that YOU can be, and you are here to show them who you are, and they are here to watch you on your time! Demand their attention! Own it!! I encourage healthy amounts of confidence, as long as you are not arrogant.

Be overprepared. I have said this many times already, but I really believe in the importance of knowing the directors, casting directors, production company, and anyone else associated with the project. Know the script, the script setting, and the materials you are performing. Bring your resume and headshot, even when they are not asked for, to be ahead of the competition. Be practiced. Know your stuff. Rehearse the audition in your head. Show them how much of a professional you are! But do not practice too much. You always want to be flexible and malleable with your performance.

Make choices! An actor who is confident enough to make choices, even if they are wrong, is attractive to a casting director. Casting directors often do not know what they are looking for. All they know is that they are looking for something unique. So commit to a choice.

Do you want to know the best decision that you can make? The most important choice that an actor can make in a scene, is to really listen to the other character. Acting is reacting. Do not just focus on your lines. Absorb what the other person is saying. Let the other person's lines influence your character's reactions.

If you have a question about the scene and what choices you should make, you can ask. However, the casting director might just respond "Do whatever you think is best." When that happens, you must decide how you are going to perform the scene. Trust your instinct and play the character how you think it should be played.

Use your personality. Your personality, your quirks, and your charms make you unique. I cannot tell you how many times I have been singled out, complemented, or cast because of my personality. Casting directors will see my YouTube channel, and when they see my "bubbly" personality, they want to cast me! Or I will go to a networking event, and after meeting me in real life, they offer me a lead role. It is so cool.

In real life, I felt that no one thought my personality was interesting or unique. But in the acting industry, my personality was valued. Hollywood celebrates *you*. Be your authentic, true genuine self. Do not try to be the perfect person, or what you think they will want. Be YOU!

P.S. I know how frustrating it is when people tell me to be myself. For the longest time, I did not know who I was. Getting to know who I was took me a long time. I have learned that knowing and being yourself mans accepting every part of you: your flaws, your interests, your humor. It is not needing to be someone else or to be perfect. It is the ability to look at the person in the mirror and say, "I love you!" Knowing yourself is a daily decision. A choice to stick with yourself, and be your own best friend no matter what.

Add Variety to the scene! In a scene where you have to yell, do not yell through the whole scene. Do not just approach the scene with one note. If your character is waking up, do not say, "I am going to be tired through whole this scene!" Real-life has layers and ups and downs. People wake up and become less tired. People get angrier and angrier, and then the emotion becomes more subdued. Try to find different emotional points and arcs in the scene.

Try to discover the humor in the scene. But if the scene is comedic, do not try to play it funny. Instead, play it seriously, as if your character is truly being affected by what is going on. Do not be a ham, or it will not be funny.

Try to find the love in the scene. Even if the character is uninterested or angry, there is always something about the other character that keeps your character engaged.

Sometimes, go against expectations. You can go quiet when someone would typically be screaming. Or you can add a laugh. Add different inflections and emphases on different words. If you are reciting a list, try to say each item in the list differently. "**Apples,** *bananas,* watermelon…"

Vary how you deliver some lines, as long as it is a believable choice.

Do not worry about the casting director. Often, casting directors will have a Super Serious Stone Face (SSF). Their SSF does not mean that they hate your performance. If you feel negativity from the casting directors, do not panic. Continue with your audition as if nothing happened. You cannot assume anything they are thinking.

Also, you are not guaranteed the part just because they seem super excited and happy about your audition. I did an audition with one casting director, and she gave me so much positive vibes. I thought I had booked the job. But I never got an email afterward.

Your goal as an actor should be to do your best. Your goal is NOT to get the part but to make the casting director a fan of you: your humility, your confidence, your professionalism, and your acting skill. You may not get the role, but the casting director will remember you. They will be more excited to call you in for projects and cast you for the next available thing they have. You want to build a good relationship with the casting director more than anything.

Thirty

How To Do Video Auditions

⁓᷍ↄ᷍ↄↄ᷍⁓

For some auditions, you will not be asked to audition in person. Instead, you will be asked to send in a self-tape. A self-tape is a video you send of yourself performing the script. Self-tapes seem simple, but they are not. Many people do self-tapes incorrectly, which is sad because it is important to do them right. If you do not follow the casting director's instructions, or they cannot see or hear you in the video, they move on from your self-tape fast.

I have made many mistakes and so, I immersed myself in learning how to send in self-tapes. I have also received instruction from Casting Directors, managers, agents and articles, this chapter is all the stuff that industry experts want you to keep in mind. It is the age of the internet, and we will all be doing more and more self-tapes. You have to get good at them.

Know that you do not need to spend thousands of dollars on sending self-tapes. If your acting is incredible, the director will never care that you used a cheap editing software. But you do need to have your lighting, sound, for them to watch your self-tape in the first place. If these things are not in place, they will distract the casting director from what they are supposed to be looking at, which is your acting.

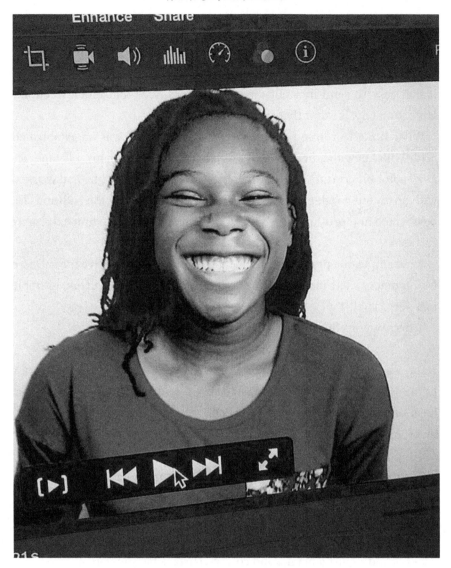

one of my self-tape auditions where my brother made me laugh

Things To Know About Location

Any random place should work for a self-tape, right? A lot of actors talk about how Lord of the Rings star Elijah Wood filmed his self-tape, as an example of the freedom they think they should have. Wood filmed the self-tape running around in his backyard wearing a hobbit costume. Is it that easy to send in a self-tape? Do actors have that much freedom? Unfortunately, it is not that simple.

What I like to remind people is that Elijah Wood was an established actor who knew the director fairly well before submitting his self-tape. He *hired* a hobbit costume and orc armor. More importantly, he had worked with an accent coach extensively for a few months before the audition. He performed and produced his self-tape at a level that made him extremely castable.

An example of a professional self-tape that you should strive for is Dacre Montgomery's self-tape for *Stranger Things'* Billy. It is THE current example of a perfect self-tape:

https://www.youtube.com/watch?v=cJ1zhq3yNBM

Dacre shot his video in his own home. You can film your videos in your home as well! Your goal should be to shoot your self-tapes with the same level of clarity and framing. As you get more money, you will want to invest in a good mic, a blue/gray backdrop, camera, and lighting, to get your self-tapes looking exactly like Dacre's.

The first step to completing a successful self-tape is having your location secured. Choose a place with minimal background noise and a solid colored background. A wall is a good place to start. Your background should be completely clear. Do not film with door knobs or windows in the background — just a plain, solid colored surface behind you.

It is highly recommended that you purchase a background. Casting director favor blue and gray backgrounds, and these colors are fairly compatible with most skin types. A plain white wall also works well as long as you wear a shirt with a contrasting color.

Do not film outside. A long time ago, a casting director requested a self-tape from me. The audition notice specified that grey was the best color for self tapes. My old house was gray on the outside, so I placed my tripod outside...and filmed my audition outside. Ugh. The tape had embarrassing wind noise. At one point, a plane goes by and ruins the audio for like ten seconds. The *only* thing done well in my audition is the gray wall. It would have been so much better for me to stay inside with my brown walls, than to film outside. I still cringe when I think about that audition.

Things To Know About Lighting

Lighting is fairly simple. Put the light source in front of you, so it shines on you and comes from behind the camera. You may want to film in front of a window where a lot of natural light comes in. You can also purchase artificial lights. Before I purchased professional lights, I filmed in front of a window, or I put a lamp in front of me to ensure I got the lighting I needed.

You do not want the light to be coming from behind you or above you. This will cast distracting shadows on your face. Stand less than a few feet away from the wall behind you. Otherwise, the casting director might see your shadow on the wall and get distracted. But do not stand too close to your wall, because you want to create some depth.

If you film in front of your window, be conscious of lighting. The clouds can cover the sun and affect the exposure. It is best to shoot when the sun is shining through your window. Do not film at night unless you have artificial lights.

Here's a super amazing article on the basics of lighting that I recommend reading before attempting to light any scene of yourself: https://www.bbc.co.uk/academy/en/articles/art20130702112136241

Things To Know About Framing and Equipment

You can get high-quality videos with a very basic set up. I have also made a list of resources and recommendations by industry experts on how to upgrade your equipment at the back of the book. But right now I want to tell you how you can create a high-quality self-tape with minimal equipment.

For filming, you need a reasonably good camera. And good news! Most people can use the outward camera on their smartphone. Most smartphones currently have fantastic cameras that are perfect for self-tapes. Now, I film my self tapes with a Canon T5I. But you do not have to invest in a fancy camera before you can send in a self-tape.

Your tripod can be basic, but do not have someone hold your camera while you film your self-tape. You can build a tripod if you do not have one. Before I got a tripod, I stacked up books, put my phone on top, and propped up my phone with a box. Eventually, you will want to get a tripod. You will also want a phone mount if you film with your phone, so you can put your phone on top and easily adjust the angles.

Set up your tripod so that you can stand for your audition. Casting directors advise actors to stand up in their self-tapes, so get a tripod that can film at your height.

Test your set up. I am in a lot of actor Facebook groups, where actors get their monologues critiqued. The biggest critique that actors get on their self-tape is that the actor cannot be seen or heard. Test your set up. Film yourself and play your video back on your computer to ensure that your audio and video works.

If you cannot be heard, here is is a link to mic recommended by an industry expert. You can connect this microphone to your iPhone for a minimal cost: https://tinyurl.com/w5gvlzr

Buying this mic, or a mic similar to this one, that is compatible with your phone/camera is essential if your camera does not record good audio. Be sure that no background noise gets onto your audition tape. Your audio has to be done well, or the casting directors will certainly discard your audition.

For the framing, record HORIZONTALLY!! Put the top of the frame near the top of your head. The bottom of the frame should end at the top of your chest near where the first button on your T-shirt would be.

Your reader should not be in the frame. Nothing else unnecessary should be in the frame. If you are filming a drama, you should shoot at a closer angle than you should with a comedy.

Casting directors suggest that you frame yourself so that you are slightly off-center. Frame your camera according to the rule of thirds, so that you can draw the viewer's attention right to your eyes. Take note of how Dacre Montgomery films his self-tape. He is slightly off-center for most of the video, and he is right in the attractive third of the screen. His frame starts from his shoulders and goes up. And most importantly, the focus is on his eyes.

Use what you have got! I film with my Canon T5i for my videos but at one point, I broke my camera. Oh, Marie. I had to use a table, a large stack of books, a wrinkled blue background, and my phone to film my YouTube videos and auditions. But it worked! I sent in a self-tape, with this wonky set up, and I booked a large role in a web series. With minimal equipment, I could still produce watchable videos.

Things To Know About Editing

The most basic movie editing software for Apple users is Imovie. Imovie comes with a Macbook for free, and you can install it on your iPhone! If Imovie does not work on your software, there are many other free editing software you can google, download, and use. PC users can use Windows Movie Maker. Apps like Magisto, KineMaster, and Lightworks Free are also good editors to look into. These basic softwares will have everything that you need to edit.

You may also need to look into video and file conversion apps. YouTube tutorials will teach you how to import files, edit clips together, export your files, and upload to different websites.

When you are editing a self-tape, keep the edits simple. All of your transitions should be a simple fade in, fade out. Cut out any bloopers. If you messed up in a take, re-film the entire scene and get an entirely usable cut. Casting Directions will often give specifications like "name your file Jane Doe - Character Name - S1". Be sure to name your movie file correctly so that way the casting director can find your clip!

When uploading an audition video of a script, do not use YouTube (unless asked). YouTube is for videos that YOU own. Upload on Vimeo, or Dropbox, or wherever they specify. I only post on YouTube if I am sending them a monologue, or if they did not specify another place. If you upload an audition video to a public site, make sure you make the video unlisted. If you publicize a script, which is highly confidential, you jeopardize the integrity of the story. Industry gatekeepers will not want to work with you.

So do not share your audition scene anywhere. Do not post the video on Facebook and ask for critiques. Do not send the script to your friends. This script is someone else's property.

FILMING THE SELF TAPE

Now That We're Done With the Boring Stuff ... here is how to film a self tape. And remember: submit the take that you are the happiest with sending.

Firstly, pay attention and follow all of the Casting Director's instructions. Video auditions often have specific instructions from the Casting Director. They may specify the background (usually blue or gray). They will instruct you on your introduction/slate, what scenes to read, how to frame the audition, editing, how to save your video, and where it should be uploaded. Read and carefully FOLLOW ALL INSTRUCTIONS.

Often new actors miss instructions, and Casting Directors will toss out the audition without even watching your audition. If you can not follow their instructions, how can they trust you on a set or in front of the director? Often less talented people will get jobs over talented ones because they can follow the process better. You do not want to be tossed! You are not a salad!!

TIP: Create a checklist of everything a casting director requires. Make a note of their tips. Often casting directors will throw in little tips such as "Be sure not to speak too fast" or "Try standing! Standing gives you more energy!" Do your best to incorporate their suggestions into your audition.

Often your self-tape will require a reader unless it is a monologue. The reader will read the other person's lines off-camera. They should stand right next to the camera, so that you can look at them and the camera will see your eyes. Look at your reader, not into the camera, when doing the scene. Only look into the camera when you are specifically asked to, like if you are doing a commercial.

Be sure that your reader speaks loud enough to be heard, but not enough to override your performance. Your reader can be the opposite gender or a different age than the character in the script. Just make sure it is not a distractible difference, like a child reading for a cop role, etc. Try to get someone who resembles the part, but if you can't, a family member or a friend will do. My aunt, my mom, my brother, and my best friends have all read lines for me. The reader does not need to act in the scene. They shouldn't be terrible, but they are just there as a placeholder for the other character's words.

Be completely memorized in your self-tape. Your goal is to recreate the scene, almost like a mini film. If the script asks for specific props, try to have them in the audition! In one self-tape I did, the other character hands my character juice and cookies. So I had my friend give me juice and cookies from off-camera as she read lines. I nibbled and drank whenever the directions said my character was eating. I did this to recreate the scene as best as I could. However, you do not have to wear the same clothing that the character is wearing. Similar to an in-person audition, in a self-tape, you can merely dress to suggest.

The lovely part about self-tapes they are self-taped! You have the freedom to prepare, make mistakes, do as many takes as you want, and give your best performance. So take your time!! Review it, and judge your performance as best you can.

The best way to review your performance is to watch your acting without sound. As you watch, ask yourself, "Do I believe this performance?" When you watch your video without the audio, you can focus on the emotion and microexpressions. Have your friends/family who are unfamiliar with the scene watch your takes without the sound. Can they identify the emotions you are trying to portray? Which take seems the most authentic to them?

Although you can do as many takes as you want, try to get it right the first time. For me, my best self-tape is ALWAYS in the first take or the last one. In my first take, I am always the most spontaneous and in the moment. Knowing this, I now rehearse and try to have my lines and props in place so I can get it right the first time. To get your self-tape right the first time, let your reader know when they need to pause, hand you your props, or complete any other directions.

If you have been filming for a while, and you are not getting the take you want, stop. Recharge. Stretch. Take a walk. After fifteen to thirty minutes, come back and watch yourself kill it. Sometimes the break is all you need. Take a deep breath. You got this.

Thirty-One

Dealing with Rejection

*t is fitting that I am writing this chapter right now, because at this moment, as I write, I am waiting to hear back on a role. Right now, I have to accept the fact that I am more likely to get rejected than to get the part. I have to admit that this is out of my control. So speaking from my current experience, dealing with rejection is so hard.

Every actor or actress faces a lot of rejection. The casting director may not give you an audition, or they will call you in and not give you a callback. Or you might get a callback, but not the part. All of these things have happened to me over and over again. An actor's entire job is just to get opportunities. Each time, you need a little luck. And luck is unreliable. So, get ready for things to go wrong.

My Story With Rejection

When I was thirteen, I came across a casting call that made me so excited. It was for a thriller movie that needed a girl aged 8-12 to play the lead orphan girl. I was thirteen at the time, but I figured that I was close enough in age to go for it.

I was called in for an audition. I had to prepare a monologue and I found a monologue that fit almost perfectly the description of the character. In the film, the orphan girl was abused, and I found a monologue where a girl talked about her abuse. The monologue was short, on topic, and it matched to film's content correctly. I could even emotionally relate to the monologue because I could draw on my experience with my dad to build my emotions. I practiced the monologue over and over.

Finally, it was audition day. I arrived at the college, found the building, and went in. I distinctly remember feeling very disconcerted because the room was tiny. Even though I was performing in such close quarters, I put on a brave face, smiled, and went through my monologue. I would say on a scale of 1-10, my performance was 7.8. It was not bad.

However, they liked it. They really did. When I finished, I remember their faces lighting up. The woman directing the audition said, "I like it. I really like it! What do you think?" She turned to her partner, who echoed the sentiment. "I like it! That was really good!" "REALLY good!" She said. I smiled and exhaled. They really liked it! I felt like I had done something unique and different. It was pretty cool. They told me, "We will be letting people know Tuesday night." Cool. I went home feeling so optimistic.

Every day I waited. I waited for that email. Most of the time, I try to forget my auditions. But I was newer to the industry at that time. I thought I would never have a role as good as this one. I was so in love with the part. And I thought that if I really wanted it, it was **guaranteed** to happen.

So I checked my email several times a day, every day. As more time past, I checked my email more and more. Finally, I set a deadline. I told myself, "If they have not sent the email by next Monday, then you know that it is probably just not in the cards for you." Well, Monday rolled around. I heard nothing.

It was the next Sunday, when they sent another email.

Hello everyone! It was so nice to meet all of you yesterday and everyone did great! We definitely have some tough decisions to make, and we have decided that the way we're going to do this is that we will contact the one/those who we feel best suit the film via either a phone call or through email by October 25.

Again, thank you all so much for you're interest in the film!

My heart rose again. "YAY!!" I thought. "I still have a chance!! They have not told the girl who got it, so maybe *I* am the girl!" I had my whole future staked on this role. I could imagine myself on set, getting into character — my very first short film, an emotional and meaty role, and perfect for me.

I prayed over and over. I checked my email frantically, my heart sinking every time my email was unchanged. Every email I got on October 25th made me jump out of my chair with excitement, thinking that I got the part. But when I checked them, they would be an email for something else.

One time, I thought I got the email, and I jumped up, yelling with my brother and his friends in the room. I checked the email and sat back down, thinking, Marie, you just made a fool of yourself. I realized then and there that if they had not sent me the email at that point, I probably had not gotten the part. I was heartbroken.

The point of that story, apart from me getting free therapy, is to tell you that rejection sucks. Sometimes you do not get the part. It will have nothing to do with your skill or work or the success of your audition. So you cannot take the rejection to heart.

We actors must get our hopes up, pour our life and soul into preparation, overcome audition nerves, and ignore anything else that day, to show up at each audition confident and ready. And then... we may not get the part. To survive in this business, you have to fend off the inevitable insecurity. You have to deal with your inner things that make you compare yourself to others. This is hard. But I believe in you. If I can do it, you can do it better. Whether the roles come easy, or they come after a 100 tries, never let rejection go to the heart. And always believe. You got this.

IV

The Acting Business

Thirty-Two

What Is A Talent Agent?

I have spent most of my time in this book talking about "How to Start."
How to start...

- Getting in the Casting Room
- Getting Your First Movie
- Getting Spectacular Headshots
- Formatting Your Resume
- Winning Over a Casting Director
- Building Your Self-Esteem & Surviving in an Acting Career

What I have covered so far could take you months and years to work out. It is so exciting how much you have learned and covered.

And maybe you have said to yourself, yes Marie, I have read every page. I love the encouragement and the information, but... How in the heck am I going to start my career if I do not have auditions??! And HOW DO I GET AUDITIONS WITHOUT AN AGENT?

Understandable concerns for sure. This part of the book is all about navigating the acting business. And this chapter is dedicated to understanding agencies, your first foray into the acting business itself.

FAQ: What Are Agents? What is An Agency?

As a brief recap, talent agents are people who work to get auditions for their talent. Agents submit their talent for casting calls. They also can act as a lawyer for their talent by negotiating contracts and handling legal interests (like whether you do nudity in a project). Agents are the middlemen between a casting director and talent. People who are looking for talent go to the agency they trust, or with a good reputation, to request talent for their project.

So, this is bad news for the newbies. Most agencies will want you to have some experience or training before they represent you. However, you can get auditions without an agent. If you are not finding auditions you need to get training, and set up your demo reels/social media profiles, before trying to get an agent.

You will likely get rejected from an agency if you submit with no experience because you are not ready. Even if the agency calls you in to audition, they might choose to reject you after your audition because you do not have enough training. An agency will probably not want to represent you unless you have an outrageously unique look, talent, or youth, or your talent is unparalleled.

FAQ: What Kinds Of Talent Agents Are There?

Before you go looking for talent agencies, you need to know which type of agency you want. Below is a general overview of different kinds of agencies. In smaller markets, like where I live, there is less speciation. Often, agencies will submit for projects in several different categories to stay in the business! Read each agency's website carefully to see what kind of work they do.

Commercial Agents: Commercial agencies specialize in submitting and booking their talent in commercials. It is easier to find representation at a commercial agency. In commercials, often the look comes first, and the acting comes second. So commercial agencies are a great place to start looking for representation.

With commercials, there is also a higher chance of being paid for your work. In commercials, it is usually a business or corporation funding the ad. Most of my paid work has come from commercials. Also, they are often looking for "everyday people" that viewers can relate too. Less experience is needed because you are not playing a dramatic deep emotional role. In commercials, you are often just acting like yourself. So for commercial work, do not overact. Just act as if you are talking to your friend, and that you genuinely love whatever product the commercial is advertising.

If you are submitting for a commercial agent, submit a smiling and happy headshot. You should also attach a clip of you performing a commercial that you have uploaded to YouTube or Vimeo as unlisted. There are plenty of commercial scripts online to find, film, and upload. This website: (http://Hollywoodactingworkshop.com/calendar/sides/commercial-copy) is an excellent place to start. There are more resources in the back.

Theatrical Agents: Theatrical agents are "film and TV" people. They submit their talent for films plays, and television. In smaller markets, "theatrical" agents will often send you out on all kinds of auditions, including modeling and commercial audition. You often need more experience when submitting for theatrical agents than commercial agents.

When submitting for this agency, try and submit a video of you doing something comedic and dramatic if they allow it. You should also submit a more serious headshot. If you can, submit with two headshots – a smiling one and a more serious one to show your emotional range. And that while theatrical agents seem the most attractive, commercials can earn you the most money. Often you should get representation from both.

Voice-Over Agents: Voice-Over work is not my focus for this book, but I wanted to give an overview. Voice-over work is "audio acting." Actors who narrate a commercial or read the lines of a cartoon character are doing voice-over work. For a voice-over agency, you will need to submit a voice demo.

Model or "Print" Agents: Modeling agencies represent models and submit them for work in magazines, clothing stores, runway shows, billboards, and more. For these agencies, you will need to have a modeling portfolio. A modeling portfolio includes pictures of you in different kinds of clothing, from professional to casual, and in different angles, varying from close up to full body shot. You will also probably need a swimsuit photo for this portfolio. You may be asked to wear something more tight-fitting in the audition so that they can get an idea of your body.

Be sure to pay attention to the following information when looking at agencies to submit for: What kind of work would you like to do? What are your strengths? Where are you willing to travel for auditions? Do you have enough experience to submit for this agency? Let this all come into play as you begin to research agents in your area.

FAQ: *How Many Agencies Can I Have?*

You can have multiple agencies if their contracts do not conflict with each other. Most actors start with an agency in a local area, and then expand to an agency in Chicago or Atlanta, and then eventually either move to LA or get an agent in LA. Actors who have an agent in LA and a local market often fly between their hometown and LA for auditions, and send in self tapes. Each agency only has jurisdiction over a specific market based on the contract. When actors have multiple agencies, they can get more jobs.

For some agencies, you can also have a commercial agent and then another modeling agency. However, if your agency represents you for commercials/theatrical projects exclusively, you cannot get another theatrical or commercial agent in that same area. After you get established in your local market, it is smart to branch out and get representation in other markets, and work your way towards representation in big cities like Chicago, Atlanta, and LA.

FAQ: *How Can I Find A Talent Agent?*

Google is your best friend. Many results will pop up by just searching "talent agencies in my city/state/nearest big city." You can also contact local acting classes, coaches, and online acting groups for their recommendations on the best agencies in your area. When you join an acting class, talk to different actors, and see who they are represented by, and what their experiences are with various agencies. Do they have good reviews? Do they represent your age? (Some agencies specialize by age, and will only represent seniors, etc.) Doing your research will be extremely helpful in compiling a list of talent agencies. More links to help you find agencies in the back.

An agency will you usually send you on auditions within an hour of the agency. When looking for agencies, consider the distance you are willing to travel.

After you have collected a list of possible agencies, it is time to create a submission list. Go through each agency's website. See what kind of talent they represent and what kind of auditions they send their talent out for. If the agency only represents voice-over actors, and you have no interest in voice-overs, remove that agency from your list.

Look at the resumes of their current talent. Do you have enough experience to be a desirable candidate, based on the other actors they represent?

After you finish compiling your list of agencies, ask your parents permission to submit if you are under eighteen. You need their full support before committing to an agency because they will probably be your transportation. They will also have to sign on your legal contracts and attend your future auditions.

You may need to explain to your parents the level of commitment and sacrifice representation requires. You will go on several auditions with no guarantee of a job. There may be commitments to long days on set, where your parents will have to be with you because you are a minor. Hopefully, through your acting classes, auditions, and other projects, your parents will sort of understand the level of commitment required. But they may not entirely know what an agency is. Tell them. Ensuring that you and your parents are on the same page is vital to your longevity in this career.

Thirty-Three

How To Avoid Acting Scams

I t is also essential for your parents to be aware because they can help you avoid scams. There are a lot of scams out there. I was eager to sign to an agency, and I got scammed. Let me tell you my story.

My Scam Story

Early on in my career, I was always researching different agencies. Before I was represented, I had a few agencies in mind and they made me very excited. Back then, I knew that I did not have enough experience or training to be represented. So I decided not to pursue representation until I felt ready.

There was one agency that I was particularly excited about. Their brand seemed super professional and exciting. They flew out many "higher-up" Hollywood people to my state, to audition the actors the agency represented. The casting directors they flew out had cast for Disney, and the agencies that came had represented stars. I also had a neighbor whose daughter was represented by this agency. The agency seemed too good to be true.

One day, I saw that the agency had a casting call. I was super excited because, as I had told my mom, this was an agency I had set my sights on FOREVER. So I submitted for the agency, and I went for their open call.

However, this audition was not what I expected. At this casting call, there was a line of kids that wrapped around the building. I knew I stood out from the others because of my experience, but it was nerve-wracking and intimidating! How had so many kids heard about this audition? There was so much competition!

For my audition, I entered this little room with my mom, and they had me read a commercial. My commercial reading was terrible. The commercial in the back of the room, and I did not bring my glasses to the audition. But they were understanding and patient as I squinted at the board to read the commercial.

After reading the ad, I handed them my resume, and they looked up my username on Casting Networks. They were very impressed with my knowledge. I knew what Actors Access was, and I had an account set up. After talking with me, they said that they were very impressed with my preparedness and research. Apparently, I "obviously" had some talent.

However, they let me know that I needed some on-camera work. And this seemed true. I had not taken a serious acting class yet, and I had gone straight from theater to film. They had a great solution – the agency offered courses to help people like me get better. They had different packages with commercial training, acting training, and modeling training. It sounded reasonable to me. But it was expensive. Even after the agent agreed to lower the prices for me down by $00, the cheapest package was $1500 all together.

I stood in that room with everything clenched. I wanted to be in this agency so bad. But I could see that my mom's head wheels were turning. My mom is strict, skeptical, and the look on her face did not look agreeable at all. I could read her – she had doubts about the price, the fast-talking agent, and the quality of the classes. But my mom only knew as much about the industry as I did. And all *I* could think about was the opportunities to meet casting directors, and talent agents. By the time I finished that audition, I could not imagine being in any other agencies but that one. My mom agreed to let me be in the agency, and even pay $300 for new pictures. But she decided everything else was too expensive and unnecessary.

For almost two years, I was with that agency, and I never booked a single job. I went to auditions for random things like a Kit Kat commercial. But I never heard anything back. And this was not because of my talent. While I was at the agency, I was constantly booking projects on my own. But in the agency, the only thing I got accepted for was a showcase, where I would be obligated to pay them thousands of dollars to fly me out to LA and be in their program. That showcase also accepted of the people who auditioned. I figured that the showcase was not worth my time. And after declining the showcase, I never got another audition from that agency again.

My first agency was a SCAM. All it ever did for me was help me to learn through "auditions." I did not realize how much they had scammed me until we declined the showcase and they completely stopped sending me emails for auditions! As much as I had enjoyed the idea of being a part of my dream agency, I began to admit that it was not for me. I had been scammed. And it took me years to realize the signs along the way.

The worst part is that I have met many actors who were scammed by this agency. One lady I talked to on set said that she and her sons had paid thousands of dollars for classes. The classes they took were useless and taught her kids nothing. Another girl I talked to had a similar experience. And yet another girl I spoke to said that she had been on tons of auditions with them that had all gone nowhere. Because the agency was so huge, it accepted so many people, and it pulled many people into its allure. A scam. Here is how you can avoid making the same mistake.

I lost a lot of time and traction with my agency. I honestly thought they were going to move my career forward, but I was able to do more for my career than that agency ever could. Be careful when you begin to think than a specific agency will make or break your career. There are scammy agencies in every part of the country, and they will try to scam you in the same way. You should be selective with your agency.

Signs of a Scam

A scam is an agency that tries to make money from actors unlawfully. Scammy agencies represent actors to sell them classes, training, auditions, showcases, etc. My agency was a scam because even though they had a few legitimate auditions, their business built on getting hopefuls to pay for opportunities.

First Sign of A Scam: One that constantly markets to inexperienced actors. Let's understand something about this business. In Hollywood, agents represent actors and submit them to people who hire actors. An agency's website should focus on showing potential hirers that the agency has reputable, trustworthy talent.

Legitimate agencies may hold open calls for "new faces" and unseen talent. But they do not *need* brand new actors. They most certainly do not excessively market to them. Real agencies are looking for talented/experienced people who can BOOK JOBS and EARN THEM MONEY. Agents get paid 15-20% of an actor's paycheck, so means they need actors who can earn them money. Legit agencies want to represent trained, talented, or experienced actors.

When agents get auditions for their actors, trained and experienced actors will do well. When they do well, the casting directors will give back positive feedback, and maybe give them a call back or the role. An audition gone well strengthens the bond between the agency → casting director, and the casting director → actor. When an agency represents good actors, it is a win-win for the actor, agent, and casting director.

So it is a red flag if the agency gears its website and marketing toward new actors. Scammy agencies will advertise that "no experience is needed" or "open to brand new talent!!" because they want brand new talent! They will have testimonials of actors on their who have had success in their company. They will focus on how they built up an actors' career, which is not normal for an agency website. Agencies focus on promoting the talent that they already have.

Scams know that these new actors are hopeful, have little experience, and are easy to scam. They will even set up their scam in smaller markets, where actors are ignorant and have fewer opportunities. Scams prey on a new actor's dream of getting discovered. Then, once they hook them, they sell them overpriced classes, showcases, photoshoots, and anything else.

Second Sign of a Scam: If an agency offers and/or pushes classes.

If any casting call, agent, manager, or casting director asks for money, run. My scammy agency offered me CLASSES, which were useless and a waste of money. Legitimate agencies accept trained actors, or they will suggest places for you to take classes. But an agency should not be selling classes, or headshots, or pushing for individual photographers.

If an agency is selling classes, they are making their money from the classes, and not from getting their actors' bookings. If they are pushing a photographer on you, they are getting a kickback from the photographer. An agent will want you to have nice, updated photos, but they will not care where you get them from, as long as they are high quality.

Do Not Ever Pay for Representation. EVER.

An agent makes money when you make money. That is an industry-standard, period. The ONLY time that you can pay an agency is for their website fee. The website fee is what you pay to be listed on their website. This is ALWAYS OPTIONAL. For my current agent, I paid to be on their website, but only after working with them for a year and knowing I could trust them.

Third Sign of a Scam: Many scammy agencies or auditions employ pressure, subtle and overt to get you to pay.

Scams reel you in with huge promises, and play on your desperation for representation and exposure. Once you are interested, they will pressure you into buying their product.

They employ many pressure tactics like constantly name dropping. The hallways of my old agency were plastered with famous box office movies, insinuating they had a role in creating these movies.

In auditions that are scammy, they will often drop names of famous people, movies and shows that they are somehow connected to. Legitimate agencies and auditions are realistic about the scope of their influence. Scammy places will make you feel like they have the power to make you a star. They make you feel like you cannot turn them down.

Scams also turn up the pressure by giving you a time limit. "You have to accept by 0:00 pm on this certain day" or, "There are tons of other people willing to accept this offer, so get back to us soon." Their words are slippery. They can be condescending, smooth-talking and more. They manipulate their words, but they never actually say what they are doing. The worst part about scams, is that they will share one or two facts that make them seem really legitimate. And they might have a semi-legitimate business going. But in the end, they are not the agency for you.

When signing with an agency, know that it should be a relatively calm, easy-going, low-pressure scenario. A real agent will understand that you need time to think, or that you can get classes elsewhere. The only pressure should come from wanting to do an excellent job in your audition for an agency.

How Do I Avoid Acting Scams? (An Overview)

1. Never give an agency money, (unless it is for a website fee.)
2. Never pay to audition (excluding submission/subscription fees for Actors Access, Backstage, etc.)
3. Remember that good agencies are selective.
4. They should not offer or make you pay for acting classes or photographers.
5. Do not pay thousands of dollars for an acting showcase. Instead, invest the money into coaching, classes, and headshots in your area.
6. Be wary of phrases like "Want to be a star?" "Want to get discovered?". Promises of money, exposure, stardom, Disney Channel, etc. are huge red flags! These buzzwords are all things to entice you, make you desperate, and make you willing to pay.

7. Be wary when they say "No Experience Necessary." A legitimate agency might represent you when you have no experience, but this phrase as a marketing tactic is concerning.

8. Do not be desperate. You <u>ALWAYS</u> have options. No agency or talent manager or audition can make you a star, promise hundreds of auditions, ensure exposure, or guarantee fame.

9. Do not be enticed by the easy route. Let the idea of "overnight success" drop from your mind.

10. Research any agency you audition for. Look for reviews. Look them up on IMDBpro and see what their previous credits are. If they do not have any, that is very concerning.

11. Be wary of what kinds of casting calls you attend, for an agency or otherwise. Most auditions for legitimate agencies will come from their website, social media, or submissions. It is likely to be a scam if it comes from a poster, a guy in the mall, or the radio saying that Disney is coming to your town.

12. If they reach out to you first, it can, but is not always, a red flag.

13. Pay attention to the specifics of what they claim to offer. They should use proper industry terms. If they call themselves a "casting agent" or a "talent agent consultant", be super suspicious. They can be using broad labels to confuse new actors on what exactly they do.

14. BEWARE if they bait and switch. If they invite you to a casting call and then try to sell you on classes, that is a huge red flag.

15. Trust yourself! Be ok with declining "opportunities" if they do not feel right. They may sound glamorous, but I can promise you that there is something better out there. Take it from someone who wasted months of her life: giving into the promises of quick success is NEVER worth the time you waste in a contract with an agent that is not doing ANYTHING for you.

16. Consider leaving your current agency if they feel off. It is better not to have an agent then to have an agent that screws you over.

Thirty-Four

How To Get an Agent

⸻❧⸻

*Y*ou need to do the following to put credits on your resume and get experience before submitting to an agency:

• Do theater and acting classes. These may be your only credits if you are in a place where acting projects are hard to find.
   • Join community theater and school plays.
   • Take improv classes. Improv is a skill that agents appreciate. Improv classes show that you have developed your ability to think quickly on your feet. They also mean that you will be more adaptable and intuitive in auditions, which agents love, especially for commercials.
   • Get your headshot and resume. Some people insist that you must have these professionally done, but not every agency requires a professional headshot, especially in smaller markets. Some agencies will only require a really good picture. In smaller markets, they understand actors may not be as experienced or have their portfolio together. However, having good headshots will give you an edge. My suggestion is to get good headshots ASAP, especially for competitive markets like

LA, but know that for many smaller areas, a really good picture is good for now.

- Take voice and dance lessons. Voice and dance lessons will help you get bigger roles in your theater productions. More significant theater credits will make your resume look better!
- Take acting classes, especially for the camera. Beginner acting classes/audition, acting for film, commercial acting, scene analysis, etc, are also good ones.
- Meeting with an acting coach once a week, either in person or on Skype, so they can work on developing your talent.
- Film yourself performing a monologue, or scene with a partner that fits your type. If the clip is filmed well and the acting is good, upload the performance clip to YouTube and use it to submit to agencies.
- Do low budget student films.
- Write scripts with your friends and produce your own movies.
- Make your social media look very professional.

Do as many of these things as you can. I did these steps over several years, starting from when I was nine. If you do not have money for one thing, do the other things until you save up enough. And always, practice at home. Practice is always free.

How To Submit For a Talent Agency?

Once you have weeded out the bad and scammy agencies on your list, the process of submission is very straightforward. Most times, agencies will have a page called something like "New Talent" or "Want To Join our Agency?" These pages will list their submission requirements. They will specify if they want you to submit via mail, email, or a website form. They will tell you what to attach in terms of demo reels, headshots, etc. and what file types to use. They will also tell you what information they need from you in terms of height, weight, contact information, clothing sizes, and more. It may be helpful to have a parent with you during your first submission process to make certain that you fill out everything thoroughly. Put your best foot forward. Give them EVERYTHING THEY ASK FOR and proofread your mistakes. Be sure to look closely at their instructions, and to follow their instructions to the letter.

Writing a Cover Letter for a Talent Agency

Cover letters are a standard part of the industry, and when you submit for most agencies, you can include a cover letter in the notes or the email. Writing a cover letter is fairly straightforward, but here are some general guidelines:

- Do not send a blanket cover letter to every agent in town. Instead, focus on the specific agencies that you have researched and would be good fits for you.
- Know your mission. Your goal is to get a talent agency to meet with you and consider you for potential representation.
- Keep your submission concise. Have a short and straightforward subject "Actress searching for representation," etc.
- Introduce yourself. They do NOT need to know your backstory about coming into acting. Explain that you are looking for representation. Tell them about what types you play, and what significant roles/and what experience you have.
- Include a few sentences about what kind of representation you are seeking representation – commercials? Modeling? Be specific. Then write one or two lines about why you would love to be a part of their agency. After I say why I want to be a part of that agency, or who referred me, I then tell them that I attached my personal information and resources.
- If they do not specify what to attach, attach 1-3 headshots, a 1-page resume, website, reel/performance clips, and professional social media. Attach materials that capture their attention.

- If you play music or have a blog, a demo reel, a website, etc., be sure to attach it! Thank them for reading your submission and bid them a good day.
- Make sure you have the correct spelling of their name, their address etc.

Dealing with Rejection From an Agency

After you send them an email, you will get one out of 3 responses. The first response is no response. An agency receives many submissions daily. If they have not responded, they may not have seen your email. The next possibility is that they got your email, but they were not interested. Either way, if they did not respond, and you are still interested in the agency, you can send them a follow-up email. However, it could be better just to consider submitting again in 5-6 months.

The second response is rejection. My rejection email looked like this:

Dear Marie,

Thank you for your interest i̶n̶ **Boring** We have reviewed your submission and we are unable to move forward to consider representation at this time. We would like to encourage you to continue your professional pursuits and build y̶o̶u̶r̶ resume. We regular post informative articles for up-and-coming talent on our blog: ̶.com. Feel free to resubmit at a later time.

Boring

This rejection came from a high profile agency in my area, and I probably did not have enough experience. But still, dealing with the rejection was hard for me. I tried to redirect my feelings of disappointment into determination. I encourage you to do the same. You should try to understand why they rejected you, but you may never know the exact reasons. They may already represent someone who looks like you, and they do not want conflicting actors on their roster. Maybe your performance clips were not strong enough, or your experience was not extensive enough.. Try to evaluate yourself and see where you can improve. Whatever it is, do not take rejection personally. If you are still interested in the agency, keep working, and submit every six months or so. Build up your credits until you get a chance to audition for them.

231

The third response that you might get is this one:

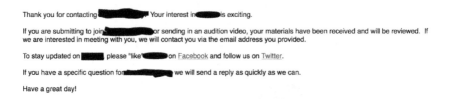

Thank you for contacting ███████ Your interest in ████ is exciting.

If you are submitting to join ████████ or sending in an audition video, your materials have been received and will be reviewed. If we are interested in meeting with you, we will contact you via the email address you provided.

To stay updated on ████ please "like" ████ on Facebook and follow us on Twitter.

If you have a specific question for ████████ we will send a reply as quickly as we can.

Have a great day!

This is great, amazing news! It means that the agency is interested in you!!! It is time to get ready.

Preparing To Audition For a Talent Agency

Agency auditions are straightforward and similar to the other auditions you have had. However, in these auditions, also come prepared to talk about your career! The agent may ask you questions about your experience, your training, your goals, and how you will be profitable to them. Prepare answers for these questions.

Practice any scripts that they send you. For my agency audition, my agent sent a list of instructions on how to schedule an appointment, what we needed to bring (headshot, resume, and a filled-out form of our information) and she gave me two scripts, including a commercial. I had to practice these scripts because I was going to perform them on camera in the audition. If they do not send you any materials, learn 1-2 one-minute monologues, including a commercial monologue, in preparation. Bring your headshot, resume, and anything else that they may ask for.

Please remember that any time you meet with an agent, you must be extremely professional. The potential agent is not just watching for your skill. They want to see how you conduct yourself in an audition, so they can know if they can send you out on auditions. Be prepared and ready to recite your material at a moment's notice. Have your reels, performance clips, your resume, and other materials prepared to present and discuss. Dress professionally and reasonably. After an audition, send them a thank you card, regardless of how it went. Even if the agent does not wish to go forward with representation, a thank you card leaves a door open for a relationship.

You also want to think about how the agency fits with you and your career. What would YOU like to gain from this relationship with your agent? Who is going to be representing you in the agency? What sorts of parts will be sent to you? What kinds of casting calls and clients come to the agents? How many people does the agency currently represent? What is the agent's policy on booking out/refusing roles/running late? What do they expect from you? What is their preferred method of communication? With my second agent, my mom also asked her: "Recommendations on acting classes and coaching in the local area? Do you ever work on casting with Disney?"

You are about to establish a relationship, and you can evaluate their ability to help you. If you are limited in your options of agencies, you may not be able to freely court and choose from different agencies, but you can at least ask questions that will help you understand more about your agency and the market.

After Your Agency Audition

Following the audition, if the agency is not interested in signing you, that is ok. I entirely empathize with your disappointment, and I encourage you not to give up. Often, in the industry, "no" usually means a "not yet" or "not right now." Take their feedback, if they have any, with a grain of salt, and keep going. Keep building your resume and training. Know that what can make one agency say no, can make another say yes. Move on. It will eventually happen.

Signing With an Agency

Hopefully, sooner rather than later, it is your time to sign with your agency. This is amazing! Congratulations, I am so proud of you. You have done a lot of work to get here. That is amazing. You have completed a ***major*** step in your acting career.

Now that you have an agent, there are few things to do. Read over any contract before you sign it. If anything seems fishy, there is a good chance it is. Always maintain excellent communication with your agent. Respond to their calls, texts, and emails. Let them know if you are running late for a project. Work hard to stay relevant and at the top of your agent's priorities. You can do this by sending them updated headshots, performance clips, demo reels, resumes, and informing them of when you have booked a job. Know that your relationship with your agent may change. You may want to move on to a bigger agency, or they may drop you. Appreciate what you have, but never take it for granted. Always be polite and never burn any bridges.

Thirty-Five

The Importance of Social Media

i asked the makeup artist to take this picture of me on set so I could share it on social media

*S*ocial Media. It is 2019, and if you are not on social media, I personally believe that you are living in the Dark Ages. There are so many talented actors and actresses I know, who disdain social media or treat it like foreign machinery. I think that this mindset is self-limiting for your success.

While social media is not necessary for an acting career, my social media presence has granted me a disproportionate amount of auditions, parts, and opportunities. People Google me and find to their surprise, my YouTube, my Instagram, and my website. They can see my personality before they have even called me in to audition. My social media also sets me apart as a small-time influencer and creator.

As actors, we need to utilize every tool that we have to set ourselves apart and make a name for ourselves. Social media is a MUST HAVE for new actors trying to establish themselves in the industry and get exposure. There are many people in the industry more skilled and experienced than you. You will need social media to set you apart.

Also, social media is how you create your first impression. Through your social media and website, people should be able to find your resume, headshot, acting clips, and special skills so casting directors can scroll through your package without even meeting you.

So What is Social Media Used For?

Social media is a tool that actors can use to get discovered and control their first impressions and brand themselves. Having an acting career is like running a business. And every business has a brand. A brand is what you are known for offering, or your passion. A business's brand is the perception the public has of that business. For example, Chick-Fil-A's brand is chicken, sauce, cows, and family. McDonald's makes you think of fries, the logo, and the Play Place. Each association is the business' brand.

Each actor has a brand → a unique set of looks, skills, and acting abilities that they are known for. What casting directors and members of the film community know of your experience, skill, looks, the types of characters that you play, your personality, make up your brand, your "package."

An actor does not need to be active on social media to have a brand. I know an actor from my acting class who is exceptionally talented. He is not very active on social media. However, he has high brand awareness because of the amazing work he does on films, and his deep connections in my film industry. Because of his talent and hard work, he is often called in to work without even having to audition for the job. He has established his reputation as a hard-working, talented actor, and people always want to buy his product.

My acting friend had to work for years to bring awareness to his brand. Use social media to market your brand. Social can be an organic way to get exposure. The more awareness an actor has for their brand, the more people may give them auditions. Social media is how you can publicize your skills as a hardworking, talented actor. You can let people in on the behind-the-scenes moments. You can also interact with other people in your network on social media. Social media is your way of putting your name on what you do, and getting your name out there.

Social media can also be used to expand your product. When someone has a significant presence on social media, they may have more to offer to casting directors. People with a large following can be asked to act in movies, even if they are not actors because people know that they can draw a crowd.

Thirty-Six

How To Get Your Social Media Together

premiere of my first martial art movie "Unknown Nation"

*E*valuate Your Social Media

Look through your social media profiles as if you were a casting director and ask yourself some questions.

- What would I like casting directors to know about me?
- Along with acting, what else am I good at? What are my interests? What makes me special?
- Does my social show my brand/type/personality?
- Does my social media clearly show that I am an up and coming actor?
- Does my social media give casting directors a castable image of me?
- Can a casting director find my acting?
- Are my profiles up to date? Are they clean and professional?

How To Clean Up Your Social Media

Now that you have evaluated your social media, you might notice that there are a few improvements to be made. Here is how to improve your social media game, start to network, and get more auditions!

First, clean up your social media sites. Delete anything shocking or controversial, on your private and public accounts. Cancel culture does not care about the difference between public and private accounts, and neither do casting directors.

Start posting regularly. A social media presence, no matter how small, is more advantageous than none. Grow your social media by posting. So start posting! Post fun, clean pictures of yourself, your activities, and your friends. When it comes to Instagram, Facebook, etc. you do not have to post solely about acting. You should mix in pictures of your acting, but you can also keep it personal.

Share pictures of you with your friends, or celebrating a holiday. Inspirational posts, interesting reflections, and funny videos are all things that are welcome on your page! If you play soccer, swim, play an instrument, speak another language, etc. post this on your social media! This will inform casting directors of your abilities and help you seem well-rounded.

TIP: Apps like Planoly and Hootsuite really help with planning and scheduling your feeds.

Get a high-quality video of you doing your special skills and upload it to IMDB, Actors Access, Youtube, Vimeo, Facebook, IGTV, Twitter, Instagram, and your website.

Make a short and professional bio. Use the link in your Instagram bio to connect visitors to demo reels, your performance clips, or your website.

Engage with others! The best part about building up social media that you can use it to connect with others easily. So reply to every single one of your comments. Use hashtags related to your career (#acting #film #modeling #yourcityname, etc.) and like/comment on the posts. You will notice your likes and followers start to grow, especially if you are posting consistently. Be sure to get a business profile on Instagram for your account, so you can track your growth using the Insights tool.

One day, I was doing was scrolling through posts under #mycityname. I stumbled across a photographer in my city, and I followed him. I looked in his bio, and his bio said that if someone was interested in doing a photo shoot with him, they should DM him. It seemed free, so I DMed him. We set up an appointment. He was delightful, and I got some fantastic pictures from that photoshoot. Social media is a powerful tool that I have used to network and create opportunities and connections for myself.

me taking a picture on a music video set for my social media

On Twitter, you can tweet the pictures you post on Instagram. Twitter is also great for quotes and tidbits about your life. Twitter is also where you want to be very careful. People like to rant on Twitter, but if a casting director scrolls through your page and sees a bunch of negativity, they will associate you with the negativity, and not cast you. They will definitely discard your profile if you have offensive content on your Twitter or any profile because they do not want their project associated with a scandal. Once you have a scandal, it is tough to get any work at all. For all of your social media, if you need to delete bad posts, do it now. And remember, even though you can delete, the Internet never forgets.

YouTube is a fantastic place to cultivate your first impression and showcase your special skills. Every actor should have a YouTube channel and Vimeo under their name. Following self-tape guidelines, you should upload well-edited, nicely shot videos of yourself onto your channels. You should have videos of you:

- Slating
- Introducing yourself/your interests
- Doing a monologue
- Doing a commercial
- Doing your special skill (like singing, dancing, etc.).

Make short films starring you and put them on your channel. Make 3-5 minute videos talking about your interests. If you are good at something, or knowledgeable about something, make videos. Be well dressed, have good lighting, and post family-friendly content. Have natural, friendly videos where you can let your charm and uniqueness show through the screen.

People may check out your Vimeo and YouTube before they check your other profiles, so cultivate your channels to control that first impression. Many industry gatekeepers see my videos months before even meeting me, or contacting me for an audition.

I am filming two projects this month. My channel helped me get auditions and book the roles for both of them. My channel has helped me connect with people in ways that no one else can. Many people can act well. What enables you to book a job are the things that make you unique.

Be sure that your social media creates a cohesive brand for you. You should have the same profile picture – your best headshot – on all of your profiles, like a logo. Update all of your socials when you have new auditions, or you just completed a new project. Create a website, which is a one-stop-shop for your resume, clips, and news — always updating your Actors Access, Backstage, and IMDB profiles whenever you have new clips or new roles.

Thirty-Seven

Standing Out In This Industry

When I started this industry, I did not think that I was unique and special at all. I thought I was boring, plain, and untalented. I struggle with those insecurities to date. How does one combat that?

Being Unique

In one of my very first auditions, I was auditioning for a group of Christian teen actors, dancers, singers, and leaders. They would travel around my city and put on performances about sexual integrity, cheating, friendships, etc. I was auditioning for the acting team. This audition was such a huge deal for me.

At that time, I was young, around 13 or 14. The script dealt with some pretty harsh teenage issues, which were out of my acting range at the time. For example, I remember having to yell the name of a genital. I felt extremely uncomfortable in that audition. I was too young, and while I was still committed to the performance, I was too innocent to take on the challenge of that acting group.

After my audition, I waited for my mom to pick me up. Somehow, I started a conversation with the husband of the company director. I scarcely remember the conversation now, but I do remember that he was "fascinated" with me. He *brought me back again in front of the audition committee,* including his wife, and he enthusiastically talked me up. He gave me his special recommendation, telling them all about how amazing I was. It was so cool! Later that week, they emailed me. I did not make it into the group, but they gave me a special invitation to come back next year and audition.

What was amazing to me was that the whole conversation did not happen because of my acting skill. It happened because I was so invested in acting that I was willing to risk rejection, loneliness, and being an outsider to come to the audition. In the audition, I was the youngest one there. Everyone there knew someone else, and I sat alone by myself, filling out my audition sheet with my mom on the phone.

But despite my novice appearance, I was also the most prepared. I had my resume and headshot (even though they did not ask for it), and I saw that many girls there did not. I had also been acting a lot longer than many of the girls there. Even though I was scared pantless, I did not hold myself back in the audition room. I presented as my most confident self.

Afterward the audition, I was open, and I talked to the guy with excitement and passion. I was willing to be different. For cool stuff to happen for you, you have to be willing to risk anything to follow your dream. My passion and excitement for acting shone beyond my talent. Who I was inside opened the door for me to connect with people and establish a relationship.

My value does not come from being like everyone else. My value comes from being me. We grow up in a culture of "never enough." Never good enough, never funny enough, never interesting enough. It took me a long time to realize that everyone is unique in a beautiful way – their own way. Tapping into your uniqueness comes from accepting yourself exactly as you are. Our differences and humanity are what make us unique, so own it, instead of being ashamed of it. You can never be replicated. So your true work is accepting yourself exactly as you are. Expressing what makes you unique. And believing that you have that special "it" factor.

Thirty-Eight

How To Network

Pitching My Script at a Filmmaker Networking Event

*A*nyone you talk to in this industry will say, "Entertainment is all about *who* you know." You need to meet other people if you want your career to grow. There are many talented actors, but those who made it were at the right place, with the right people, at the right time.

Right now, your primary goal may be getting auditions. But even getting auditions is hard without connections. Casting directors only put 30% of auditions on public audition websites. All other film roles are filled through connections: agents, managers, casting directors, directors, and people who knew the casting director. To start getting auditions, you have to start making connections with people.

Your future agent and manager are some of your major connections. They have access to casting calls that will never reach the public. By being signed with them, you will get access to more auditions. Sometimes you can get a job through your connection without even having to audition.

As I write this, my agent has just booked me for a Macy's Fashion Show. I did not have to even audition for it. I was just lucky – I only *happened* to be connected to my agent, who has this connection with the lady who ran the yearly Macy's fashion show. I was in the right place at the right time. That is how the industry works.

As you go on more auditions, you will also gain more connections and build relationships. If a casting director likes your audition, or you film a movie with a director, people may remember you and your acting, and ask you to audition for other roles. They become a connection. You establish relationships in the industry through months and years of work and networking.

Using Social Media

When you are starting in the industry, social media is how you can make connections. Research actors, filmmakers, YouTubers, directors in your area and find who you want to work with. Follow these people on social media, and interact with them! Show genuine interest in their work and interests.

During my first year in acting, I spent an extensive amount of time looking up lists of local production companies, groups, websites, Facebook groups, and Twitter/Instagram accounts. I created my own Google Doc to list each company and person, and I followed them all. When I joined an acting class, I followed all of my friends from the acting class online. I joined as many Facebook groups as I could. Interact! Being mutual friends/followers is the first step to establishing a relationship.

I began keeping up with what they were doing. I commented on their posts, asked questions, and generally engaged. On Instagram, I follow casting offices and like and comment on their posts. I will subscribe to them on YouTube and comment on their videos. Twitter is great way to interact with business and professionals, and I will start or join in conversations.

Often if someone follows me back (like a local photographer, manager, or director), I interact with them on their page. Sometimes I will join them on Instagram Live! My actions may sound very Machiavellian, but I approach every person in this industry with genuine interest. I will talk to you whether or not I know you can offer me something at the moment. I try to see how I can help others, and I focus on being a supportive community member. I understand that no matter what someone can give me, relationships are the real currency.

Once in a while, during my interactions, people will click on my bio. From there, they would see my YouTube channel and learn about me and my journey with acting. Soon we became mutual supporters of each other's work!

Sometimes I will just be striking up a conversation with someone, and they will ask me to come in and audition for their newest project. Social media has become a very organic way to make connections and network. Before you know it, you can be networking with the industry professionals in your area without ever leaving your house!

What Not To Do When Networking

- Never ever do these grave networking mistakes:

- Never harass a casting director or industry professional (or... anyone??). Do not use social media to dm and pester industry professionals for auditions or jobs.
- Do not DM professionals and tell them or even ask them to check out your website or other social media profiles. <u>Do not</u> ask them to follow you back.
- Avoid asking them for random feedback or asking random questions.
- Follow the guidelines of any acting Facebook Group you are in.
- Do not tag casting directors in random pictures, or leave annoying comments.
- Do not be purely selfish. People can tell. The best networking happens when you ask "What can I do for them?"
- Do not, *not* be strategic. Although you should not be selfish, be aware of what each person can bring to you.
- Do not submit for casting calls over social media.
- Do not use social media to ask questions about an audition that you are submitting for.

Your job on social media is to interact – support and be consistent, but do not be annoying. Build a community.

(me and my wonderful friends from acting class)

Networking Locally

After about a year of connecting with people on social media, growing my following, and getting more mutual friends on Facebook, I began to develop a network. As I auditioned and did more films, I added more people to my network.

Once every few months or so, someone would message me about my YouTube channel. I was building relationships. This was a very slow process. I learned that often, it was the people who worked with me before who called me back or booked me for another role. At the time, I did not realize that I was "networking," and that was a side effect of networking.

After a year or so, these connections begin to pay off. People started adding me to acting Facebook groups that were invite-only! These groups gave more access to casting calls and networking events. Interacting and connecting with others, birthed more chances to communicate and connect

253

with others.

One of the opportunities I got in these groups was an invitation to a local "Filmmaker Actor Director Meet and Greet." So at fourteen years old, I brought my headshot, made business cards, and handed out my information to filmmakers and casting directors at the meet and greet. As a kid, I was gathering courage and learning about how to approach and network with adults decades older than me.

I learned that people are open to meeting new people and supporting others' passions. I made connections that continued to grow after we added each other on social media. I eventually started a Networking event group for young actors and filmmakers in my area. Because I did this so young, I realized that if I could do it, anyone can do it at any age.

my old business cards with baby Marie

Later, everyone in the group got invited to a local TV channel launching. The channel was going to stream the content of local filmmakers and creators in the area. The event was going to have a red carpet and a banquet. The invitation listed no age restrictions, and so I figured I was completely welcome at the event. However, I was definitely the only fifteen-year-old at the banquet.

At the event, I got my picture taken ON MY FIRST RED CARPET ever. Afterward, someone introduced me to the guy in charge of MAKING the TV CHANNEL (and the whole event). The guy was so excited about me, and the stuff I did that he took me to meet all these executive bigwigs.

All of a sudden, I found myself in an elevator surrounded by three or four very tall men in suits. I was young, and I did not know how to handle this situation, and I put my foot in my mouth. But my awkwardness never took away from the gravity of the moment. I had gone from being added to a group, to a red carpet, to meeting the executives of a TV channel. How did I get here? I was not more qualified than anyone else. Was I that resourceful, passionate, smart, and determined? Or was I just lucky? All I know is amazing things happen just by showing up.

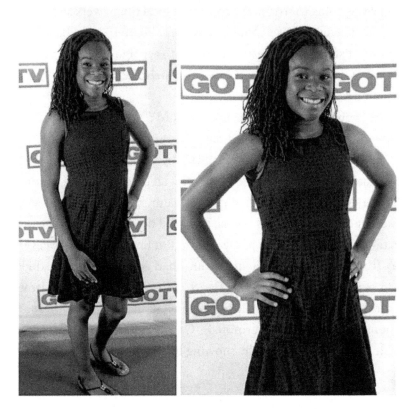

me at my first red carpet event in June, 2017

The whole night went much better than I expected. I met so many filmmakers and handed out my card to everyone. I met one author, who wrote a novel and a script. She was looking for a girl my age and race to play her younger self. I completely fit the part. We exchanged information and eventually connected over social media.

That night, I also met an amazing couple who does so many cool things in my industry. The husband has been in well-known sci-fi movies, and his wife produces and self-distributes films around the Midwest. They own a film studio together and have made a lot of really cool movies. To this day, we are still connected on Facebook, and we support each other's work.

Now, because I have networked for such a long time, I often work based on connections that I already have. I have worked with the same film production company on three of their different films. I did a lead role in a paid docu-drama this year, and the director who hired me knew me because she was the audio recorder on the project I had done previously.

Work begets work, and the longer that you work in this industry, the more work you will find coming up. It takes a lot of time and patience, but you did not expect this to be easy, did you?

Thirty-Nine

The Art of Making Connections

Me and Sharee at a Filmmaker Conference

*T*here are a lot of really cool people in this industry. I really want to tell you all about one special person I connected with, because her story inspired me, and she taught me a lot about networking. Sharee Silerio is a local writer, film and TV producer. She writes articles on mental health (see: https://sincerelysharee.com/) and is currently creating a video series on black women's mental health. She is a wise, sweet, smart, compassionate woman, and I am so glad to have met her.

My mom suggested I should connect with her. I reached out, and of course, in my message I attached the link to my YouTube channel. She watched my channel and told me she had advice that she would love to share it with me. We launched into a conversation and we had so much in common. She gave me wonderful advice for my acting career, my channel, and getting started in the local industry. She offered her knowledge and expertise. She opened herself up, and told me I could reach out to her, if I ever wanted to chat, and I am forever grateful. I eventually interviewed her for my channel!

me on my interview with Sharee Silerio

I want to encourage you guys to reach out. Unsolicited messages to casting directors and others can be extremely off-putting and that is why I think this could be the most controversial advice I have given in this book. You could do more to hurt your reputation than help your career. But by following my gut and reaching out to a few select people, I was able to open doors that I did not think was possible.

Also, people love to share about themselves. Sending a few respectful messages and questions to someone in the acting industry about their experience can launch into the most extended conversation. I think reaching out is be important, as long as you have a couple of things in mind.

People are really nice and often open to helping others, as long as you are professional, respectful, and reasonable. If you are polite and reach out without demands, you can be proactive in making your own connections. Respect their boundaries. Do not text them a "hey what is up" every day.

I have had many people message me, asking me questions, and most times, you guys are SO FREAKING SWEET. But sometimes, I get that message from that person with a sketchy profile. The message asks me for private details about my life. The messager is entitled asks me to do all of their research FOR THEM. This kind of communication is unacceptable when communicating with anyone in the acting industry.

Do not talk to people you do not know as if they are your friend. Do not pester them, pressure them, or get into arguments with them. It is an extremely small industry, and incorrect behavior with one person will be remembered by many.When messaging, do not use incomplete phrases, rude/casual replies, send off-putting questions, or have an entitled attitude. People are often polite if you are polite, but if you are not, they blow you off.

On the flipside, know the value that you bring to any interaction. You do not want to be overly polite. When I was younger, when I met 'important' people, I would try to be excessively respectful, and then I would bomb the conversation. For example, one time, the producer of my 2016 Superbowl Commercial came to the set during filming. The commercial was already a pretty big deal to me. I had also done a whole bunch of research on this company and found out who this person was before I even met him.

So, I completely amped him up in my mind, and I tried WAY TOO HARD when I was meeting him. I tried to overcompensate to seem worthy of this pedestal that I had put him on when he was just a regular guy. What I wish I had realized is that everyone is a human being. I do not have to put myself down in my mannerisms or self-respect, to feel "worthy" of someone's presence.

How to Make Yourself Lucky

Sometimes the person who gets the role is not the most qualified, but the one with the most connections. None of the four girls in my Super Bowl commercial had to audition. There were hundreds of girls who would have died for our parts, but the girls with me on set did the ad for fun. They got in by a family member who worked for the company or a friend. I got cast through my contact – my agent. By my luck of having that agent, I got my hugest role, and I did not even audition for it. There is no formula for success in an acting career. It takes talent, networking, hustle, and...some luck.

You can make yourself luckier. I am going to tell you guys how by giving you guys a secret acting tip. You will probably not hear this from a professional. This is something that I have learned from my years of attempting to figure out the industry.

Acting is all about increasing your opportunities. You have to put yourself in places where opportunities come to you. Put yourself out there and be vulnerable and expose yourself to uncertainty and rejection. Sometimes you have to put yourself in places where you are not wanted.

When I first started acting, I submitted for casting calls that asked for eighteen-year-olds when I was fourteen. Now I would never submit myself for something so entirely outside of my age range, but I learned valuable lessons. I learned what was in and out of my acting range. I booked parts where I was supposed to be a college student as a highschooler. I have been on film sets where they assumed that I was 18+, and the raunchy college students exposed me to a lot.

So many times on set, I was way out of my depth, but I wanted to be there more than anything. I learned so much. And I would never have gotten those credits, or those auditions if I had limited myself because of my age. Of course, this form of risk-taking does not always go well. And I am not recommending that you submit yourself for parts that do not suit you, lie about your age, and go on film sets where you are not wanted. I am saying have initiative and expose yourself. Put yourself in uncomfortable situations to get the part.

Make mistakes and learn from them. Early on in my career, I got advice to go to my local colleges and film schools and hand out my headshot and resume. I do not have many film schools locally, and I did not have a ride to local colleges, so I did the next best thing. I searched for every college in my state. I found their media/communication/video department, and I emailed my headshot and resume and Youtube channel to them. It was a long shot, and I knew it. I got crickets in response. That was definitely a mistake. But mistakes are ok to make.

I tell these stories because I believe that all of my stories are tied back to being unique, and following yourself and your dreams. I was often the youngest teenager in the room, always putting myself in situations where I was doing something that I had never done before. I have driven on set without a permit, I have lied about my age, and I have showed up to places where no one expected me to be. I have made a lot of mistakes, but in making mistakes, I did the right thing.

The initiative, that willingness to risk everything, that is what makes you unique. The universe responds to those leaps of faith. You have to be willing to be the youngest, to be the most alone, the most 'crazy'. You know what you want. You have to accept what you want and go after that. And every day, I am still learning that.

As I end this chapter, I am going to let you in on a little secret. I have been writing this book for four years, and every time I read over each page, the same thoughts come to mind:

"I am not qualified to write this book. I am a nobody in this industry, and I have nothing to offer people with my writing."

Thoughts of judgment from those who pick up my book and shame from the acting community flood my mind. My anxiety is amplified by the fact that no one I know is writing a book. While I was writing this book, my friends were watching TV, or doing homework, or socializing, or sleeping, like a normal people.

Now I am 18, and all of my friends are doing college internships or getting high, or doing college applications, or traveling abroad. It's 11:21 pm, and my head tells me I should not do this. *"Why am I here? Everyone doubts that this book will ever make it out. This is really hard, and I should just give up."* Everything in me tells me I am not good enough, that I do not deserve to be a successful author, that this book cannot help anyone... that I do not deserve to be here.

But... there is a little voice back there in my head. My crazy voice. My crazy voice is the voice that gets me into crazy situations. It tells me that I can accomplish anything. My little voice was validated and amplified by the support of my family. My voice said that this book could really help people. It said that if I believe in it, my stories and knowledge can change someone's life.

So I am going to write this book anyway. It is the process of being crazy, staying up late every night doing the hard thing, and being willing to be different that leads me to success. And it is the same thing with acting.

There are going to be a million reasons why you should not pursue this career. They will sound like: "You are not good enough. There is too much competition. You are too late. You have no money", and anything else you can think of. Trust me, I have thought of them all. But if you are willing to risk the pain, if you are willing to be insane about it, if you are willing to give everything up because you love it, there is no reason that you should not do it. Listen to that little crazy voice in your head. Be insane.

Forty

Answering Your Frequently Asked Questions

*H*ere I am going to answer the most common questions that every actor, manager, talent agent, and Hollywood expert gets about the industry every day. These questions also come from the sentiments you guys have left on my channel. This is a summary of everything that you have learned in this book. I have added some insights into the same themes that I have attempted to let resonate through this book. I wanted to add this chapter to make simple what I have taken hundreds of pages to explain. An acting career is simple, but not easy. Focus, prioritize, and you can navigate it easier than you think.

Before I start, I want to give a thank you to anyone who has ever left a comment, dmed me a question, or supported my career overall. You guys have inspired me to make it this far. We are nearing the end of the book, which means I am nearing the end of my time with you. I sincerely hope that I have helped you. I have shared with you guys everything I know, and a little more. I am so thankful to be able to do so. You all are my happy place. Without further ado, let answer some questions!

Your FAQS

Hey Marie. My passion is acting. I have had a love for acting every since I was five years old. I love standing up in front of people and entertaining them. My dream is to be in film and television. Do you have any tips or advice for me?

Hi! It is so lovely to meet you. Congratulations on finding out your passion! Acting is a beautiful, challenging, and creative craft. Because of this, acting requires actors to be strategic.

My first suggestion is to make clear for yourself what exactly you want to do. Do you want to be in the theater? Do you want to be on film? Do you want to be on television? Do you want to be on commercials? Where do you picture yourself most vividly when you close your eyes? Your answer to these questions will determine your career choices and focus.

Then, research and learn precisely what you need to do to achieve your dreams. Make a step-by-step blueprint plan to get there! Create a vision board so you can see clearly where you are going. Then base your activities around your specific dream. If you are drawn to the theater, you need to put yourself in plays.

If you want to do musical theater, take dance and voice lessons along with your acting classes. As you get older, your plan should include moving to a place like Chicago and New York to pursue theater. If your goal is film, you may want to move to Atlanta or LA. Spend your time learning from other actors' stories. Many actors have interviews and stories about how they made it. Although everyone has a different journey, their advice will help you create your game plan.

Once you know what to do, do not second guess your plan. Go after it.

My biggest regret in my acting career is that I spent years second-guessing my choices, fearing the hard work, and doubting if success was possible. I wasted time and lost many opportunities because of my insecurities. If you are looking for a sign, or a perfect time, this is the sign. You can do this! You have your goal and your plan, so believe in yourself commit and work your butt off.

Belief in yourself is crucial to your success. It is impossible to commit to a dream if you do not believe that you can accomplish it or that you deserve to have success. So go to therapy, do positive affirmations, watch inspiring speakers, but DO NOT waste years of your life in fear of failure. Learn to abolish doubt and to trust that little voice inside of you that says you can do it.

Hi Marie! I loved your video! My passion is to be an actor or actress. But it's really hard where I live because I live in the middle of nowhere. There are never any opportunities/agencies where I am. Could you please help me or give me some tips for building up my resume?

Hi!! It is very nice to meet you. Thank you so much for leaving a comment. I truly understand how you feel. I also live in the middle of nowhere, and there were not many opportunities for me here at first. So, I had to create my own opportunities. I joined the local film and acting Facebook groups, and followed every director, producer, creator that I could on Twitter, Insta, and YouTube. Then I used my YouTube channel to create films, publish my monologues, and market myself.

The best way to succeed is to create opportunities where there are none. Go to your local college and hand out your resumes in the film department. Publish monologues and generate a following. Practice on your own. Do low-budget films. Raise money for acting training. Network online. Try and move to a big city as soon as possible, but in the meantime do what you can. If all you can do is watch TV and practice scripts at home, work your butt off and do that.

me filming one of my earliest short films "Sacrifices"...the lip color...whew chile

For the longest time, I despaired because I felt like my entire acting career was dry spells. Sometimes I would only audition once or twice every three to four months. I fretted over my lack of opportunities. Getting an agent and using social media helped. I also started getting more auditions when I quit martial arts and took responsibility for my own acting career. I stopped waiting for opportunities to come to me, but I made time to go after them with full force.

But know that as a beginner, or in a small town, sometimes you have to wait a long time before you can simply **GET** an audition. There are some seasons with many auditions and some seasons with none. Every actor goes through it. Have patience. It takes five to ten years before you can be established in the acting community. No matter what happens, do not give up because there is always a better bus coming.

Hi Marie! I love a passion for acting and singing. But will the fact that I am black/so tall/have braces/have braids stop my acting career. Should I try or just give up??

The amazing thing about living in 2019 is that people are so open to diverse casting. In the past month, I have come across two castings for dark-skinned teen girls as lead roles in huge studio movies. In movies and television, you can now see people with all kinds of hair types and looks everywhere. It is amazing. Your dreads, braids, braces, your skin tone, whatever it is, can set you apart and make you castable.

However, being unique means that when casting directors want a more familiar look, or have a specific look in mind, they might not want to cast you. Casting directors will state what they need in the breakdown. If the description excludes you or includes you, it has nothing to do with your ability to be successful in the industry. If casting directors want a girl with braids specifically, they will specify that in the breakdown. If they do not want braids, they will say "no braids" or "natural hair." If they do not care, they do not specify.

The important thing is to be yourself. You may not be able to change your braces or ethnicity. The most important thing is to be yourself, own who you are, and work hard. Because when a casting director is looking for your look, you will be the best one in the room. And then you will book the role.

If you are worried that they will make you cut your hair (or permanently alter another facet of your appearance), you have to decide what you will do next. For most student films and low budget films, they will not ask you to alter anything. On bigger productions, they might ask you to shave a beard or dye your hair. Often for those big projects, you will be compensated for your trouble. If the changes still do not work for you, you can always choose to decline. When you decline the changes, it is up to the filmmakers to decide whether to move forward with casting you for the project.

Conclusion

This is it! You have now reached the end. I never would be finishing a book right now. I gave myself a deadline, and guess what, Marie? It is 11:54 at night, and I am finishing it. I think me writing this book as a good analogy for starting an acting career. This book started as a dream, a passion, something I wanted to do. But the goal was far away, and I was not anywhere near close to a finished product.

To complete my goal, I began to take small but consistent steps to move me forward. I did some research. I outlined. I did more research. I reworked the outline. I compiled all my thoughts. And then I began writing over and over and over — day in and day out. Till 3 am on school nights, I wrote. While falling asleep, while refusing fun outings, under the wildest circumstances, I wrote this book. I spent hours writing, visualizing success, overcoming obstacles, and committing to finishing this book over and over.

And finishing this book is the most fulfilling thing ever. I am beyond happy that right now. I fulfilled my dream. The hardest part was never writing. It was overcoming myself. And it is the same for you.

My last instruction for this book is that you give back. I wrote this book because I wanted to help you guys in the same way my mom, Wendy Alane, and my other mentors helped me. I worked hard to give you guys a product that would change your career. I encourage you guys to do work that helps other in the same way. The most important thing in life is touching other people. So I hope I touched you. Thank you so much for reading this book. I appreciate you so much.

Above all, I thank God. God has given me everything I needed to succeed. In my every dark moment, he has been right there. He gave me everything I needed for happiness - my life, my talent, every opportunity I have had, and the people in my life who support me, and every single one of you. I thank God for everything I have and everything I will have. I will continue to thank him in the good times and bad.

I hope you guys accomplish your dreams. Until next time, ciaoo.
Marie Tagbo

Online Resources

If you are looking at these resources in the paperback version, check out this Google Doc, with the new links to all of these online resources.
https://tinyurl.com/wvsweb2

Agencies

What Does A Talent Agent Do?
  Wikipedia on Agents
  Samuel French's Yearly Compilation of Agencies
  SAG-Aftra List of SAG Franchised agencies
  How to Get an Acting Agent By Rawaan Alkhatib
  How To Get a Talent Agent
  Writing a Cover Letter to a Talent Agency by Jesse Daley
  12 Steps to Writing Good Actor Cover Letters to Talent Agents
  https://www.liveabout.com/writing-cover-letter-to-talent-agency-16367

Audition

Backstage Experts Answer: What Should Actors Wear to Auditions? By Rebecca Strassberg
  What to Wear? 10 Do's for Your Next Audition by Scott LaFeber

Here's a Producer's Perspective On How You Should Audition!

Breakdowns / Casting Calls

How Not To Write A Casting Call by Lynne Marie Rosenburg

Breakdown Services

Actors Access
  Backstage
  Casting Networks
  LA Casting

Callbacks

21 Secrets To a Successful Callback by Matt Newton

Casting Assistants

What is a Casting Assistant? Get in Media

Cold Reading Technique

10 Ways to Master the Dreaded Cold by Matt Newton
  Mastering the Skill of Cold Reading by Clay Bank
  How to Be Amazing at Cold Reads and Nail Your Next Audition?

Commercials

What is an Industrial or A Commercial?

Commercial Scripts
  (on Google Doc)

Demo Reel

Wendy Alane, the Hollywood Talent Manager on Demo Reels:
  https://www.youtube.com/watch?v=FeQEdRs07VE
  https://www.youtube.com/watch?v=aveRW36Yty0
  https://www.youtube.com/watch?v=3uaLH0ZrYyg

Diction and Enunciation Practice Exercises

http://plays.about.com/od/actvities/a/enunciation.htm
  http://www.write-out-loud.com/dictionexercises.html
  http://m.wikihow.com/Enunciate

Headshots

7 Tips for Better Headshots by Matt Newton
  How to Find a Great Commercial Photographer by Aaron Marcus
  Commercial vs. Theatrical Headshots by Marc Cartwright
  Bad Headshots, Good Headshots
  What Makes An Effective Headshot _

Monologues

10 Tips to Choose the Best Monologue For You by Eirian Cohen
  10 Tips for Choosing Your Audition Monologue by Melissa Hillman

Monologue Resources

(On Google Doc)

Objectives

What is An Objective?

Resume

What Belongs on an Actor's Resume? By Rebecca Strassberg
   How to Format Your Acting Resume and Headshots by Michael Kostroff
   How to Format Your Resume by Matt Newton
   Exactly How to Format Your Resume for a U. S. Market by Marci Liroff
   5 Unbreakable Acting Resume Rules by Deb Mcalister
   How To Make an Acting Resume by Actingislitmylife
   How To Properly Format Your Resume by Wendy Alane Wright
   Daily Actor Resume Template
   Starter Resume by Bonnie Gillespie
   More Templates

SAG

Official Website
   Steps to Join
   How Do You Join The Screen Actors Guild? By Nicole Pomarico

Self-Tape

Your Guide to a Perfect Self-Tape by Cori Hundt
   10 Tips for a Winning Self-Tape Audition by Joseph Pearlman

Christopher Nicholson's Articles (Writer/Director Advice)

(On Google Doc)

Critical Self-Taping Tips to Get You More Auditions by Wendy Alane

- https://www.youtube.com/watch?v=7tW66KxBOaQ
- https://www.youtube.com/watch?v=FqPFUroJ6pY

Slating

How (Not To) Slate for Film Auditions
   Backstage Experts Answer: How Should Actors Slate? By Rebecca Strassberg
   How to Slate for On Camera Acting Auditions
   How To Slate in an Audition

Sound Recording

Wikipedia: https://en.wikipedia.org/wiki/Presence_(sound_recording)

Websites for Actors

Best Websites for Actors Just Getting Started

What Did You Think of The Book?

First of all, thank you so much for purchasing my book **How I Became A Teen Actor.** *I know you could have picked any number of books to read, but you picked this book and for that I am extremely grateful.*

*I really hope that it added at value and quality to your everyday life. If so, it would be really nice if you could share this book with your friends and family by posting to **Facebook** and **Twitter**.*

If you enjoyed this book and found some benefit in reading this, I'd like to hear from you and hope that you could take some time to post a review on Amazon. Your feedback and support will helping me to greatly improve my writing craft for future projects and make this book even better.

You can follow this link:

https://www.amazon.com/d-
p/B081MC6KFX/ref=cm_sw_r_tw_dp_U_x_XPT1DbQ3X5AYW

to the review page now.

*I want you, the reader, to know that your review is very important and so, if you'd like to **leave a review**, all you have to do is click **here** and away you go. Please be honest I wish you all the best in your future success!*

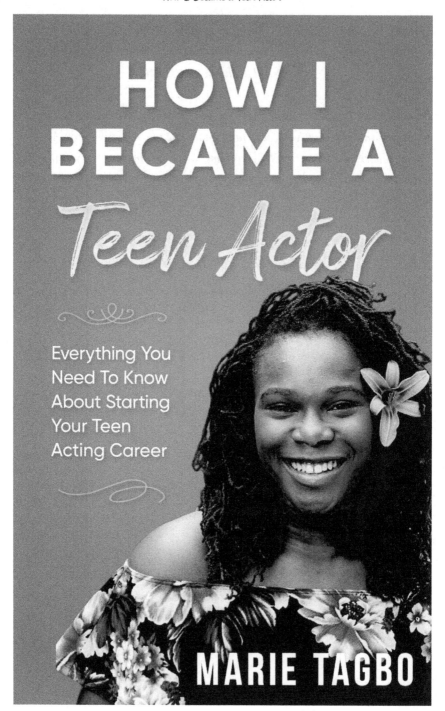